WikiBeaks

TRANSWORLD IRELAND

Penguin Random House Ireland, Morrison Chambers, 32 Nassau Street, Dublin 2, Ireland
www.transworldireland.ie

Transworld Ireland is part of the Penguin Random House group of companies
whose addresses can be found at global.penguinrandomhouse.com

Penguin
Random House
UK

First published in the UK and Ireland in 2017
by Transworld Ireland
an imprint of Transworld Publishers

A CIP catalogue record for this book
is available from the British Library.

ISBN 9781848272446

Designed by Bobby Birchall, Bobby&Co.
Printed and bound by Printer Trento, Italy

Penguin Random House is committed to a sustainable
future for our business, our readers and our planet. This book
is made from Forest Stewardship Council® certified paper.

MIX
Paper from
responsible sources
FSC® C018179

1 3 5 7 9 10 8 6 4 2

DUSTIN'S
WIKIBEAKS

EXCLUSIVE FILES FROM IRELAND'S
FAVOURITE SUPERSTAR – REVEALED!

Contents

ZIG AND ~~ZAG~~ ZOG

Foreword by Zig and ~~Zag~~ Zop

When Dustin told us to write a Foreword to his book we were delighted as we had no idea he could read, let alone write. So, we decided to support our famous feathered friend with his new book or, as he likes to say, 'me buke' as in 'How many copies of me buke are yis buying, Zig and ~~Zag~~ Zop?'

We've known Dustin for many, many, many years and he's really nice and all most of the time but he can be really annoying too. When Ronan Collins won him for us at a December golf match we thought he'd only be around until Christmas Day, but here we are almost ~~thirty~~ 13 years later and he still calls in asking what we're making him for dinner!

We had lots of fun with Dustin on *The Den* most of the time, until he started taking over; using it to run his ~~dodgy~~ brilliant building business, his ~~dodgy~~ deadly taxi business, his ~~dodgy~~ music career, his dodgy burger business and his ~~dodgy~~ inspirational political career . . . not to mention his ~~dodgy~~ Eurovision Song! We even got ~~stung~~ to pay for the bill from Tesco for his Eurovision shopping trolley which he ~~dumped~~ kindly donated on our lawn!

What really persuaded us to write this is when Dustin told us that he was doing this book to say sorry for all he put us and Ireland through. But just in case, anything mean he says about us, Demo,

Ray or Zuppy probably ~~isn't~~ **IS** true. However, anything he says about Ted, Podge or Fergus the Astrologer is probably spot on!

Just a couple of things we felt were important to clear up before you read this book (which Dustin refused to show us before badgering us to write this bit!)

1. ~~Zag~~ **Zog** is my name, not Zog as Dustin always called me.
2. We ~~never~~ applied for British citizenship!
3. Zuppy is well. He now lives on a friendly farm in Meath.
4. Zig and RTÉ weather woman Jean Byrne ~~aren't~~ **have** 'a thing'.
5. ~~Zag is not~~ **Zog** a gold member of Ryan Tubridy's book club.

We do hope that Dustin prints all this and ~~doesn't~~ write**s** any silly comments over it. He assured us he ~~wouldn't~~ **will** as he's ~~not the same turkey he once was.~~ *exactly the same as he's always been.*

So finally, all we'd like to say is: congratulations, Dustin, on writing this impressive book and we hope that you, dear readers, will enjoy a trip down memory lane with the ~~second~~ most famous Dustin Hoffman in the world and Ireland's favourite turkey!

PS. Do **Not** hang on to the receipt~~, just in case!~~

Love

Zis + ~~Zag~~ *Zog x*

DUSTIN
ME EARLY YEARS

Congratulations on buying this buke. It's probably the best thing you'll do all Christmas. And congratulations again if you're reading it too, it's definitely the best thing you'll do on the jacks this Christmas. Unless you're a fan of Brussels sprouts; then it'll probably be the second-best thing you do on the jacks this Christmas.

The good news is that this isn't like most autobiographies. I won't prattle on for three chapters about how me grandparents met. (It was at a Joe Dolan Christmas gig in The Noggin Inn. They were on the menu but set free by an angry vegan – is there any other kind?) The truth is, my family have and always will be the people of Ireland and especially the boys and girls who first made me a megastar when I revolutionised TV back on *The Den* with Ian, Ray, Damo, Francie, Don Conroy, Simon Young, the two Zog boys, Zuppy, Socky and Ted. They were happy days and full of fun, long before Ray D'Arcy declared his War On Craic, when he still had hair and went to Mass with his 64 brothers and 48 sisters every Sunday after he'd woken them up at 6am to play 'The Rose Of Tralee' on the melodeon for three and a half hours. So yeah, a good while ago now . . .

People thought we just made it up as we went along on *The Den*. They didn't think we had meetings and rehearsals and they were spot on – we didn't . . . and that's where the magic was. That and the fact that the clowns running RTÉ had no idea we were even on; they were far too busy banging out

Zag was clearly as thick as a pigeon, Ian wouldn't hurt a flea and Zig . . . well let's just say Zig had a fondness for stationery, especially brown envelopes.

Ray takes his orders from me

RTÉ's Head of Human Resources meets me on my first day

brutal telly for grown-ups to even know that their kids' stuff was pure gold. If even one of the bearded cardigans that ran the gaff had spotted the level of craic we were having, you can be sure he/she would have had us taken off air straight away.

I remember me first day in *The Den* like it was the Tuesday last week. As everyone knows I was won in a golf club raffle by Ronan Collins around Christmas 1991 – not the best time for turkeys. Famously tight-fisted, Ronan thought I'd make a great Christmas present for someone else, but his wife made clear I wouldn't be an appropriate gift for her. So he handed me over to his pals on *The Den*. I wasn't so keen but once I met the gang I knew I'd a chance at surviving. Zag was clearly as thick as a pigeon, Ian wouldn't hurt a flea and Zig . . . well let's just say Zig had a fondness for stationery, especially brown envelopes.

It was a simple task then to take over the show. First up, I told Ian that if he played his cards right he could be the next Marty Whelan but he'd either have to grow a moustache and dye his hair purple like Marty's or quit kids' TV and be taken more seriously. He was gone the next day. The Zog lads were harder to shift but in the end Zig's love of dosh over everything else saw them do a Zexit and leg it over to Britland to take the Queen's shilling. They spent years earning millions by telling Chris Evans he was great every morning.

With *The Den* now my own I hired Ray D'Arcy, Socky and Snotzer Galligan as me support act and the rest is golden telly history. I went on to become a global megastar, living it large with loads of babes and dosh. Socky became a catwalk model, Snotzer is in the 'Joy and Ray eventually got his own Saturday night show where he gets to interview George Hook every three weeks about what he's been doing the previous two weeks. It's gripping stuff.

Two Brits and a mullet

PADDIES INTELLIGENCE GROUP

KGB, CIA, CIE . . . all superpowers have elite secret service agencies that keep citizens safe. In Ireland this highly trained unit is as secretive as it is brutal. Known to only the most senior members of Government, WikiBeaks can reveal here for the first time that this group, who operate under the name The Paddies Intelligence Group (aka The PIGs), have for decades been answerable to no one as they use their remit of 'keeping Ireland safe from bad people who do bad things to good people' to spy on anyone they wish.

Searching through the mountain of secret files (four) from The PIGs we've come across some shocking dossiers compiled on individuals felt to be 'risks' to the nation's security. This list includes all midland TDs, Bono's hairdresser, all Healy-Raes, Geraldine from D.I.D. Electrical and those two ginger kids from that John Hinde postcard with the donkey.

Shockingly, the list also includes a number of international names from the world of politics and religion. Names such as Nelson Mandela (the former pillar from O'Connell Street), sax (sic) fan Bill Clinton, and Winston Churchill, the famous dog from the insurance ads.

Our key mission at WikiBeaks is to expose the truth, so we are proud to release these files.

MOTHER TERESA OF CALVITA

Name: Mother Teresa AKA Mammy T

Aliases: Mammy T, Honey T.

Date of Birth: Year Dot

Place of Birth: Las Vegas

Eye colour: Purple

Hobbies: Avid tea towel collector; All Calcutta Grand Theft Auto champion 1994–97; Motherwell season ticket holder.

Heroes: John Bishop, Des Bishop, Bishop Eamonn Casey, John the Baptist, Clare Daly TD.

Known Associates: Pope John Paul I, John Paul II, John, Paul, George, Ringo, Mattress Mick, Conor McGregor, Jesus, Dame Judi Dench.

Known Nemeses: Sister Sledge, Twisted Sister, Scissor Sisters, Midge Ure and Satan.

Favourite Food: Caviar, Monster Munch and Kebabs.

Most likely to say: 'No man needs two coats when one man has no coats'; 'My house is your house'; 'Who Let the Dogs Out?'

Least Likely To Say: 'Would you like to see my tattoo?'

Drives: Yellow Honda Civic Turbo, go fast stripe, '92 Cavan reg complete with 'My Other Car's a Rickshaw' bumper sticker.

PIG

In Dustius We Trustius

TOP SECRET

Born to Nun

Background Notes and Key Connections to the Republic:

Mammy T left home aged 16 and didn't return until later that evening with a packet of Monster Munch. Unfortunately her entire family had moved, so with only her prized packet of Monster Munch, she decided to move to Ireland. There she auditioned for The Loreto Sisters, a savage all-girl group who were wildly popular at the time.

After a few years gigging, The Loreto Sisters finally called it a day and Mammy T was faced with a dilemma: go solo or become a saint? In the end she opted for sainthood but luckily, while in Calcutta she maintained several links with the business community in Dublin. She owned a 35% stake in Lillie's Bordello, a string of Spar shops on the Northside and was on the board of Spin FM. Not all her ties were purely business and in 1996 she co-funded a medical centre for Northsiders. Called Dr Quirkeys, this centre has been at the forefront of medical advancement in the north inner city and became world famous for its treatment of Senator David Norris's accent in 2007 where it managed to reduce it from 'ridiculous' to 'just a bit gas'.

Records show that Mammy T also maintained close personal links with Ireland via friendships with some of our higher-profile citizens. This was not something she wanted to bring attention to so, cleverly, when she organised Vogue Williams' hen night she arranged that they would all dress up as nuns.

Though Mother Teresa is widely believed to be dead, the PIGs have not ruled out a persistent rumour that she is in fact currently living in Moate and working in an Applegreen.

Bray

THE LAND THAT TIME FORGOT

If Wicklow is the garden of Ireland, then Bray is the bit of compost you hide down the back of the hedges beside the rotting garden shed. The river Dargle flowed through the town for centuries. However, the announcement of water charges saw locals drain it. This has led health officials to speculate that many Brayers may soon wash.

Bray train station opened on 10 July 1854 with the first train arriving in June 1953 and causing panic amongst locals who feared that the gods had sent a giant dragon to punish them.

In 1998 the Tour de France passed through Bray. It was hoped this would boost tourism to the town. However,

after doping tests showed that 87% of the spectators were on banned substances, and the fact that locals robbed 57 bikes, an ambulance and Lance Armstrong whilst they were racing up the main street, the estimated visitor numbers failed to materialise.

In 2011, it was revealed that officials at the Department of Foreign Affairs sent pictures of people from Bray to the British Government in an attempt to persuade them that the Sellafield Nuclear Plant was having a negative impact on this east coast town. Twenty-three British officials who saw the images were granted early retirement and given full counselling and psychiatric support.

Bray's Field of Dreams

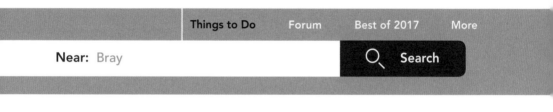

| Things to Do | Forum | Best of 2017 | More |

Near: Bray

🔍 **Search**

Europe > Ireland > Province of Leinster > County of Wicklow > **Bray Tourism**

Bray Brighter Homes Exhibition 2017

Tax 'efficient' Dutch rocker Bono moved into the town in the early 80s. After a short stay, he decided he'd have more chance of saving Africa than Bray so he legged it back to Amsterdam.

Bray has the biggest Asian population outside of Beijing, so much so that the town is known in China as Brayjing. Local Jimmy Chung O'Toole said: 'When I first arrived here I thought they were reenacting Michael Jackson's "Thriller" video, but sure it was just the locals out shopping.'

In 2009, Dara O Briain pipped other locals, Laura Whitmore and Katie Taylor, to the title of Miss Bray. It's a title he retains to this day despite rumours he's had breast implants. While Dara and Laura have earned enough money in their careers to move on from Bray, Katie Taylor decided to stay because she wouldn't get as much fighting practice anywhere else in Ireland.

The Irish for Bray is Bré (pronounced Bray) because the locals aren't the brightest and at least they would have one word *as Gaeilge*.

Bray Air Show brings over 250,000 spectators to the seafront to watch delayed Ryanair flights fly through clouds on their way to exotic places like Glasgow and East Midlands.

Brayjing

EDUCATION
People in Bray are learning German so they
can start shopping in Aldi and Lidl.

PASTIMES AND HOBBIES
Nose picking and appearing on *Crimecall*.

TWINNED WITH
Chernobyl (though Chernobyl is appealing).

COUNTY
Thinks it's in Dublin the same way Kilkenny
thinks it's a city.

HOPES FOR THE TOWN
Kim Jong-un could push the button.

POPULATION
The O'Byrnes, O'Tooles and O'Chungs.

The Dargle, Ireland's Blue Danube

*Home to Braveheart, Penny Dreadful and Celebrity
Jigs'n'Reels*

*You know a town's in trouble when the McDonald's is
the nicest building around*

COMMENTS

Q Search

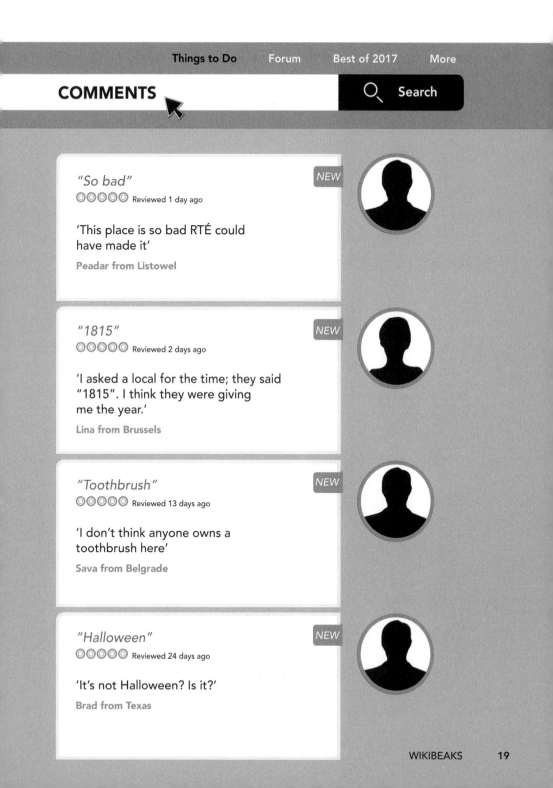

"So bad"   NEW

◎◎◎◎◎ Reviewed 1 day ago

'This place is so bad RTÉ could have made it'

Peadar from Listowel

"1815"   NEW

◎◎◎◎◎ Reviewed 2 days ago

'I asked a local for the time; they said "1815". I think they were giving me the year.'

Lina from Brussels

"Toothbrush"   NEW

◎◎◎◎◎ Reviewed 13 days ago

'I don't think anyone owns a toothbrush here'

Sava from Belgrade

"Halloween"   NEW

◎◎◎◎◎ Reviewed 24 days ago

'It's not Halloween? Is it?'

Brad from Texas

RTÉ*GUIDE*DOGS

Knit your own bone

Winalot of puppy toys

The Cavan Rose reveals her bran-based way to fitness

Dunphy looks back at some of his old looks

Blathnaid Ní Woofach: Madra Maith

Spot the dog competition

'Síle is a Pedigree Chum,' says Gráinne

AT HOME WITH THE SPICY GINGER

With her giant tongue hanging out of her huge mouth, a clearly excited Blaithnaid Ní Woofach comes bounding down the path as she spots us. Her tail wagging at a rate that would power a small island, she barks excitedly at us and all of a sudden it's like we're in an old Lassie movie as we run after her and arrive right outside her brand-new Dermot Bannon-designed kennel.

Beaming at the front door, she proudly welcomes us in. We're the first visitors to be allowed inside since Dermot convinced her to add on a glass-box extension. 'I wasn't sure at first as I'm a deeply private dog and don't like attention, so the thought of others being able to look in when I have friends like Mary Kennel-y, Brian Kennel-y or Sinead Kennel-y over for a few bowls of water after one of our legendary runs had me worried. Mary is especially thirsty after a good run; at 237 (in dog years) she's not as light on her feet as she used to be, unlike our Brian who could outrun the rest of us in a heartbeat, especially if there's another dog's arse to be sniffed.'

Rumours

Eager to dismiss tabloid stories about being inbred, the Meath native claims her pedigree is 100% Red Setter, adding, as she wipes away a tear, that just because her grandparents were cousins doesn't make her any less of a Red Setter. We hand a clearly upset Blathnaid a tissue. She looks us straight in the eye as she bows her head, cocks her leg and lets rip an almighty dog fart that lasts a good 40 seconds and reminds us of our recent visit to the Galway Arts Festival.

'I'm fierce kennel-proud'

They say every dog has its day, but it's clear talking to the shiny red setter that this madra isn't ready for hanging up her lead just yet. As she talks excitedly about her new project, a six-part series for RTÉ1 called *Where's Gráinne Seoige Now?*, it's hard not to like her and obvious why she is without doubt the nation's second favourite Red Setter, after the one on the side of the Bus Éireann buses.

POSTCARDS FROM THE EDGE

ROME
Dear Dustin,

Greetings from Rome, where the Romans lived in the Roman era before they went roaming. The streets here have names which is really handy. Bono was once in a place where the streets had no names and it was a total nightmare to get around – a real health and safety hazard, that.

Have to head out now. Bono's saying Mass later in St Peter's and the Pope's been on looking for two tickets. Larry says he has to pay for them.

Ciao, Edge.

PS: I'm going to ask the Pope for one of his hats. I like hats.

DUSTIN MEGASTAR

THE NOGGIN

IRELAND

Washington DC
Hi Dustin,

How are you? We're in Washington today and I'm REALLY bored. Bono's off meeting politicians and talking to the news channels about whatever it is he's prattling on about this week. Also it's a U2 Haircut Week; ya see it really suits Bono as he's got the same hairdresser as Donald Trump. Bono says the guy's a genius, a 'Hair Artist' he calls him. Larry says the lad's a 'Hair Terrorist' who should be charged with Crimes Against Heads. Larry's very funny like that, always cracking jokes – like when we go for meals out and when the bill arrives he takes it and says things like, 'I only had water and one onion ring'. We all laugh and then Bono pays.

Your pal, Edge.
PS: As we're surrounded by politicians here I'm gonna get a new cowboy hat. I like hats.

NEW YORK
Hi Dustin,

A big howdy-doodie from New York! New York! So good they named it after that diner in Tullamore. Bono let Larry sit up front on the tour bus and he gave the bass player (Alan?) a shout-out from the stage for his birthday. Never seen him look so chuffed.
I went to the Museum of Science with Stephen Hawking. The bass player (Andy?) went to The Museum of Modern Art with Banksy; Larry to see The Yankees with Conor McGregor; and Bono went to Wall Street with his accountants.
Doing The Today Show on NBC tomorrow – it's ages since we met Dáithí and Maura. Bono got new stabilisers so he's going to cycle down from Wall Street, a street that has a name, which is funny because mostly here the streets have no names, just numbers.
Stay cool, Edge.

DUSTIN THE TURKEY

DUBLIN

IRELAND

PS: Got a new hat. I like hats.

Here at WikiBeaks we are proud to release the truth behind TG4's viewing figures which were previously only known to three people in TG4, two members of The Hothouse Flowers and ginger chancer Hector.

It was when *Ros Na Rún* decided to shock viewers with its first non-inter-family wedding storyline that I decided to take a closer look at the deeply unpopular bogger soap that goes out on the underground crusty TV 'channel', and stumbled across the top secret audience data.

The *Ros Na Rún* 'viewer'

The move to feature the wedding of two characters who are not related was met with outrage from the show's loyal audience, known to his friends as Padraig. Padraig was so angry he sent a strongly worded fax to the producers urging them to reconsider airing the episode. Responding to Padraig's concerns, it was when executive producer Síle Ní Seomrasneacghtaagusbuachailliisteachanteach Óg asked, 'What's a fax machine? Is it one of them modern telex yokes?' that Padraig decided enough was enough and the time had come for him to become a whistle-blower, contacting us here at WikiBeaks Towers with the shocking news that he was the soap's only viewer and that was mainly because his telly was broken and stuck on TG4. Padraig can't even speak Irish.

Defending the show's position Miss Ni Seomrasneacghtaagusbuachailliisteachanteach Óg pointed out that the storyline had given *Ros*

Na Rún its highest rating since the station went on air in 1876.

Our research confirms this fact as the controversial episode made history when it became the first time the soap had more viewers than cast members, with ratings rocketing into double figures. *Ros Na Rún* employs 34 people and that night won an astonishing audience of 37, with three more people watching on TG4+1.

The 37-strong audience makes the non-family wedding episode the sixth-highest rating broadcast in the channel's history, with the top five highest ratings belonging to *Police Academy 4*, *Police Academy 7*, *Police Academy 3*, The Queen's Visit To Ireland and the 2014 Massey Ferguson ad.

These figures confirm that the bog-based channel costs €23 million per viewer per year, a figure that is set to rise dramatically as Padraig has recently had his telly fixed.

Not Overheard

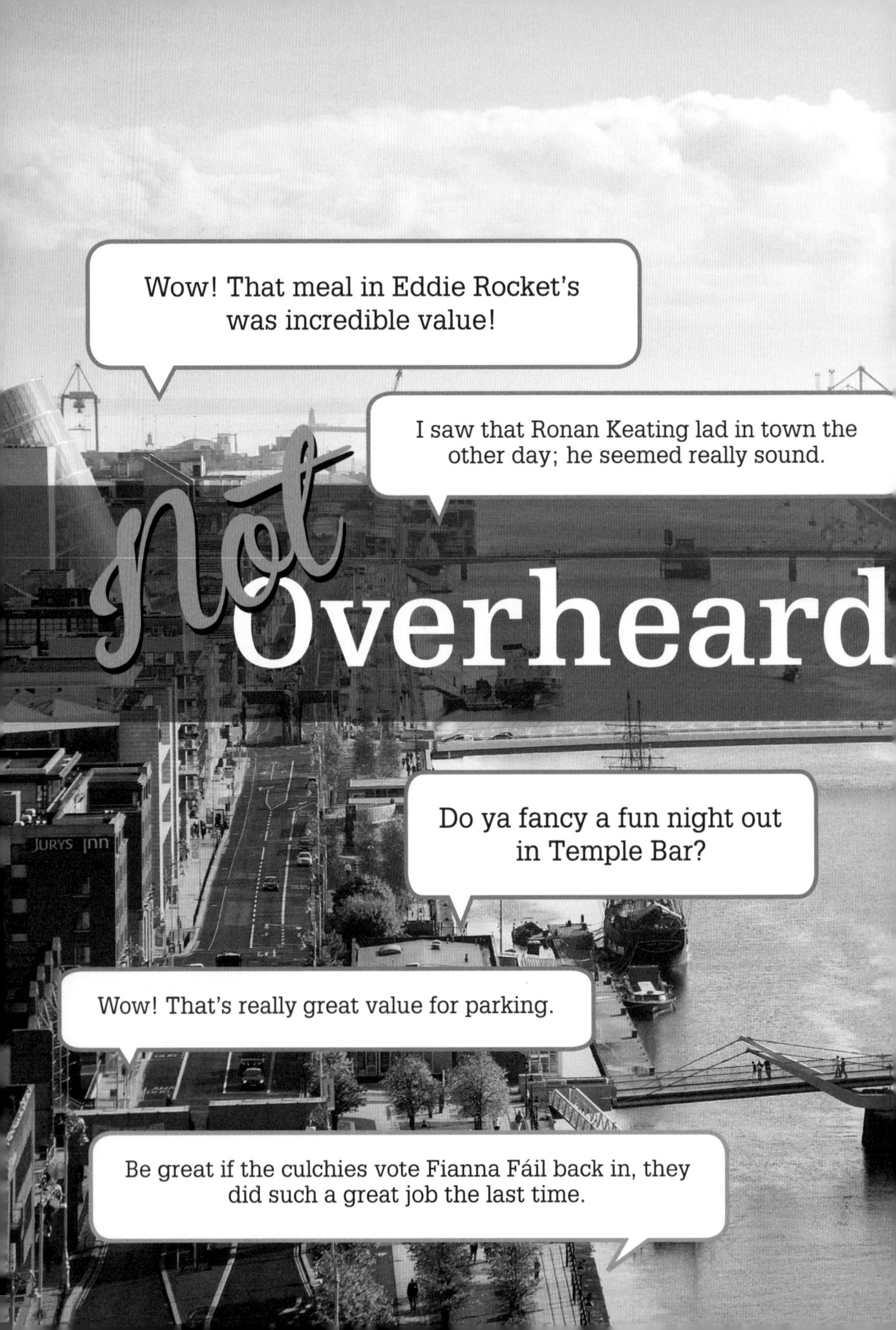

It's such a shame The Gooch has retired . . . I'm devo for Kerry GAA.

I really love U2, but The Edge is such an annoying prat . . . Bono's really, really cool though.

In Dublin

Fingers crossed *Riverdance* will be back in The Gaiety this summer.

Hey listen, thanks for clamping my car; you guys do such great work . . . is there any way I can add a tip to my payment?

Hi! I'm going to see a movie in Screen 4, just wondering if you've any watered-down Coke and some overpriced popcorn?

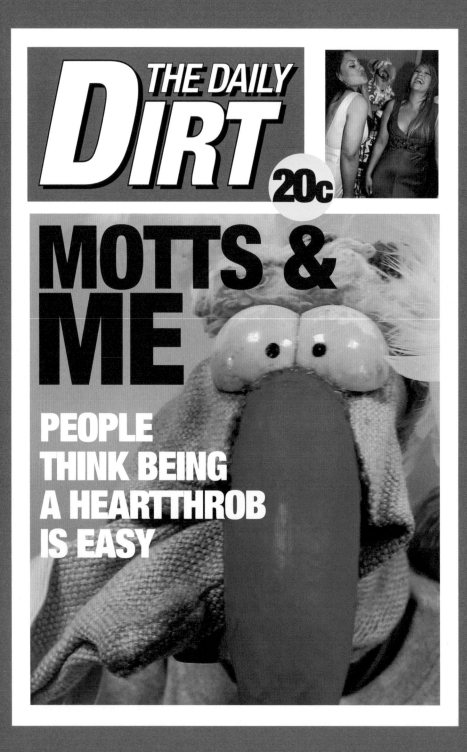

THE DAILY DIRT

20c

MOTTS & ME

PEOPLE THINK BEING A HEARTTHROB IS EASY

'I'M NO MATTRESS MICK,' SAYS DUSTIN

People think being a heartthrob is easy. They think being desired by millions – and in my case, billions – of women worldwide is fun. They think you have it all just because beautiful women will do anything to please you. What they don't realise is just how sad and lonely it is to be seen as just an object, a thing of great beauty to be drooled over. But I'm someone with feelings and a brain as well as unbelievable good looks.

Don't get me wrong: some lads love it – just look at Mattress Mick. I've been linked to many of the world's best-looking motts but, trust me, motts can be hard work. That's not to say I've not from time to time cashed in my celebrity for nights of passion, but I'm no kiss'n'tell bird. What happened in Room 347 of The Heritage Hotel in Portlaoise in May 2014 with Kim Kardashian will remain top secret. You'll not see me selling my story to some tabloid about her particular 'tastes', and anyway, so what if she likes Knickerbocker Glories? What a grown woman chooses to do with jelly, ice cream and a megastar turkey whilst dressed up as a Traffic Warden in the privacy of her junior suite is her business and her business alone.

And while it goes against my gut, the publishers of this book have insisted that I spill the beans on my love life and as they're paying me a serious three-figure sum to write it, I'm contractually bound to do so.

> **I've been linked to many of the world's best-looking motts . . .**

So within these pages, you'll find all the gory details on my three most memorable conquests.

THE DAILY DIRT

15c

AMANDA WAS MY FIRST LOVE

Amanda Byram mid-fart

MY NOGGIN LOVE-NEST WITH MANDY

Amanda was my first love. She got me long before all the other girls. She saw me for who I was and not just as an opportunity to get into a video with Joe Dolan – she really was one good-looking woman. As a kisser she was very tongue-heavy, but better than her sister.

After I gave her her first big break she promised me that I'd always be her man. We secretly moved in together in the Noggin. The first four days were magical but after the initial honeymoon period, the rot set in. You see Amanda is a lot of things – kind, gentle, smart, funny and hot – but she's also a dropper of some of the worst farts I've ever smelled/tasted. Honestly, she's the face of an angel with the arse of a docker. Imagine a combination of the bang from that dog food factory in Longford and a Brian Cowen eighteen pints of Guinness fart and you'd be half way there. It wasn't the smell, it was the creepy celebratory way she'd release them. I will never forget the morning I woke to her bum hovering inches above my nose as she let rip a huge one while singing 'Come Out Ye Black & Tans'.

I knew then something needed to be done so I got her a gig on *Ireland AM* so that she'd be gone in the mornings and I could sleep soundly knowing I'd not be woken in terror.

The first of Mark Cagney's 42 TV wives, Amanda quickly became a favourite with viewers who couldn't smell her work. After two years of holding their breath the gang in TV3 couldn't take it anymore and Amanda was sent back to me. By that time I'd moved on to loads of other motts, many of whom never woke me with a fart, but as I knew she had a thing for funny lads I decided I'd help set her up with a comedian. None were available so instead I hooked her up with Nordie spoofer Patrick Kielty.

Once in Britland with Paddy she took the brave move of sorting out her farting and after a six-week stay in The Priory Clinic she emerged fart-free and ready to take on the world. With the speed of a Galway lad running to beat closing time in SuperMac's, Amanda landed huge shows on Channel 4, BBC 1, ITV and Sky before heading to America where she hosted *The Swan*, a show that featured Amanda interviewing famous swans. I like to think that her golden years with me helped her empathise with these less majestic birds. All these huge shows have now given Amanda the confidence to step on to the big one as she finally got herself on to RTÉ1 where she presents *Dancing with the Stars* with her nephew and world-famous mime artist Nicky Byrne.

HOW TO SPEAK TO A NORDIE

ABIGWATABOUTYEWEEMAAAN

Nordies are a funny lot. The Brits don't want them, we don't want them and they don't want each other. But on the plus side, Spandau Ballet and Simple Minds did write songs about them, so every cloud . . .

Not an alien

The main problem with Nordies has nothing to do with history or politics. It's that no one can understand a word they're saying. No one knows how Nordies ended up speaking the way they do but some experts have studied it and come to the conclusion that it's because of the influence of Julian from UTV, who many believe is an alien sent to Nordieland from Jupiter to make the rest of them appear normal.

For anyone thinking of heading to Nordieland to get some . . . eh, 'fireworks', I've compiled a handy phrase book to help you understand all the Ivans and Seamuses you'll meet along the way.

ABigWhaddAboutYa: Hello.

ABigWhaddAboutYeBigMaaan: 'Hello' to anyone over four feet tall.

ABigWhaddAboutYeWeeMaaan: 'Hello' to anyone under seven feet tall.

YeOffDownTeSuperCrazyPrices? Are you going to the supermarket?

DoYeWanChopsWiThhhaaaat? Would you like chips?

WatYouCrayOnAboot? What are you crying about?

WindYerNeckIn: Please take your head back inside the car.

Windy: The day before Thursday.

Freestaters: Normal people.

Ulster Fry: Stephen Fry's Nordie cousin.

TraditionalRoot: Anyone's back garden.

Norn Iron: Northern Ireland.

CatchYerselfOn: Cop on.

Shittyation: Everything.

Wee: Small urine.

Aye: Yes.

AyeNo: Yes No.

NoAye: No Yes.

Noooo: No thank you.

TheBritsAreComin: There's visitors on the way.

AchNo: No.

BelfastBap: A bread-based bun.

A CHIP   A CHOP

Nordieland has a wealth of attractions for visitors. There's the world-famous Titanic Museum where Nordies have once again turned tragedy into opportunity as thousands flock to see the place where the unsinkable ship was built and set sail from on its maiden voyage in 1912 before it hit a large ice cream and sank in the Atlantic.

The *Titanic* isn't the only link Nordies have to building incredible vehicles as in the 1980s they built the DeLorean car which they proudly boast has yet to sink off the coast of America. And of course, no mention of their great manufacturing history would be complete without mentioning the steel- and iron-workers who in the 1950s built Eamonn Holmes. Eamonn has also never sunk off the coast of America but he has frequently been hit by large ice creams.

The most popular visitor attraction in Nordieland is without question the world-famous Buttercrane Centre, where shoppers from around the globe gather to stare in wonder at their House Of Cards, Poundland, Sally Hair & Beauty, Dunnes and Yankee Candle Store. Famous visitors have included Princess Diana, Nelson Mandela, Dame Judi Dench, Will Grigg, Calum Best, Dora the Explorer and Philip Boucher-Hayes.

A COLOGNE FOR THIN-SKINNED SENSITIVE SOULS

[REDACTED]

BY

DENIS O'Brien

AFTERSHAVE LOTION

Moate

RHYMES WITH GOAT

The river Brosna used to flow through here, but in 2004 decided to detour itself, finding the town way too dull.

When Michael Jackson came to Ireland in 2006, he made Moate his home for seven months, saying the locals reminded him of his best friend Bubbles. It was also very easy for him to reenact his 'Thriller' video by just walking up the main street with the residents on a busy shopping day.

They say all roads lead to Rome, but unfortunately some roads lead to Moate, County Westmeath. The place should be done under the Trade Descriptions Act; there's no moat and not much else of note in the town. As you approach the town you are met with a bang of blandness, which continues right into the centre of this kip and only lifts when you see the sign 'Thank You for Visiting Moate – Come Back Soon!' At least that shows the locals have a sense of humour.

Historians say Christopher Columbus discovered Moate in 1494, but rather than having to live with the embarrassment of an association with the town he jumped on a boat and tried to sail off the edge of the earth.

Michael Jackson's 'friend' Bubbles, who blended in well with Moate locals

Parts of the movie *The Great Train Robbery* were filmed at Moate train station in 1979. Locals still love trains and enjoy nothing more than hanging around the station's platform waiting for them. As the station closed in 1987 many go home disappointed but remain hopeful enough that they return without fail each morning.

The latest reviews. **The lowest prices.** The perfect place . . .

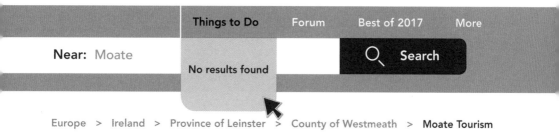

Things to Do   Forum   Best of 2017   More

Near: Moate

No results found

🔍 **Search**

Europe > Ireland > Province of Leinster > County of Westmeath > **Moate Tourism**

The Monte Carlo of the Midlands

The Two Euro Shop on the Main Street doubles as the local estate agent.

Moate's first internet café was due to open last year, but locals protested outside because they didn't want to catch 'any of them viruses'.

Neighbouring towns are fundraising to have an actual moat dug around Moate.

PASTIMES
Pastimes in the town include bingo, eating out of bins and licking cars. Music was last heard in Moate in 2004 when a visiting Dub had 'Crazy Frog' as his ringtone. Moate also proudly lays claim to its title as the Cousin-Scratching Capital of Europe.

POPULATION
Between 1,500 and 3,000. The population of the town halved in July 2014 when 1,500 brave men and women started the long walk to Croke Park to see Garth Brooks. News never reached Westmeath that the concerts had been cancelled, and the whereabouts of the missing pilgrims is unknown.

NIGHTLIFE
Bingo and Supermac's

INDUSTRY
1,423 blacksmiths, 36 bingo callers, 17 cobblers, 9 switchboard operators, 5 bus conductors, 4 town criers, 3 scarecrows, 2 witch doctors and a bloke who walks in front of a car with a flag.

If you only visit one farm store this year . . .

kipAdvisor®

EIRCODE
ZZZzzzzzz.

PLACES OF INTEREST
See Nightlife.

EDUCATION
A copy of *Soundings*, on the Leaving Cert between 1969 and 2000, is shared around the town.

SPORT AND LEISURE
See Nightlife.

FUTURE
Talk of being twinned with Nairobi has locals excited whilst locals in Nairobi have reacted with mass hunger strikes.

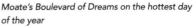

Moate's Boulevard of Dreams on the hottest day of the year

Locals are always excited to see each other

Who needs Disneyland?

COMMENTS

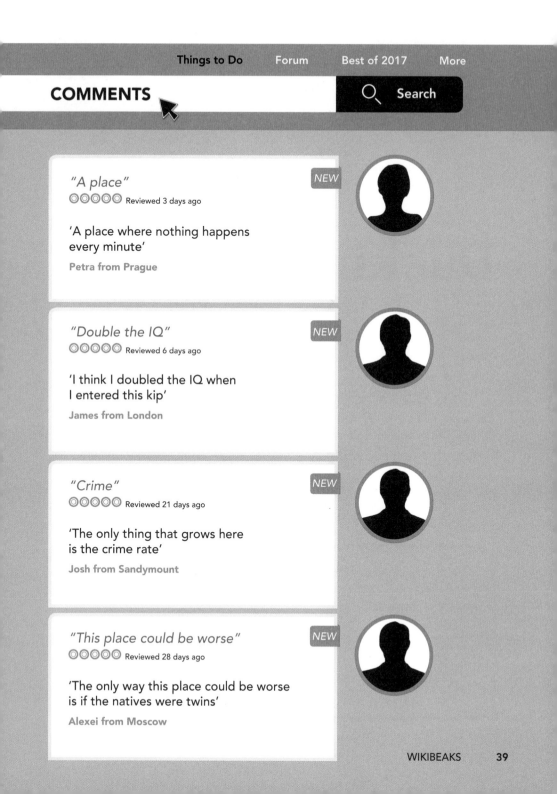

"A place"
◎◎◎◎◎ Reviewed 3 days ago   NEW

'A place where nothing happens
every minute'

Petra from Prague

"Double the IQ"
◎◎◎◎◎ Reviewed 6 days ago   NEW

'I think I doubled the IQ when
I entered this kip'

James from London

"Crime"
◎◎◎◎◎ Reviewed 21 days ago   NEW

'The only thing that grows here
is the crime rate'

Josh from Sandymount

"This place could be worse"
◎◎◎◎◎ Reviewed 28 days ago   NEW

'The only way this place could be worse
is if the natives were twins'

Alexei from Moscow

Ducking Donald

Donald Trump is the President of America, though things are moving so quickly that by the time me beak stops tapping out this sentence that may no longer be the case.

For this book to feel bang up to date the publishers asked me to write down me thoughts (as a previous Presidential candidate meself) on 'The Donald'. They also asked me to write them in the summer for a book that in the main won't be open in most houses (jacks) till 27 December, so I've come up with a cunning way of writing it in the summer but having it feel like breaking news at the same time. Ladies and Gentlemen, I give you the world's first multiple choice political essay!

Looking back on 2017 I think it's fair to say that everyone will remember where they were the day President Trump
- ◯ Was impeached.
- ◯ Was shot.
- ◯ Said something smart.
- ◯ Didn't embarrass an entire nation/planet.
- ◯ Pressed the nuclear button when he was trying to order a pizza.

It was weirdly surprising and at the same time totally predictable as only the week before he'd managed to
- ☐ Offend an entire religion.
- ☐ Announce he was invading a country that didn't exist.
- ☐ Finish a whole sentence.
- ☐ Make Sean Spicer look smart.

Obviously at the time most right-thinking people thought
- ☐ 'This is hilarious! Where can we watch more of it?!'
- ☐ 'Oh no, the world is about to end.'
- ☐ They were dreaming it all.
- ☐ 'Jeez, his wife looks like a lizard. Is his wife a lizard?'

But as the year rolled on everyone got used to the fact that
- ☐ Sean Spicer had stormed the White House briefing room, killing the President and the entire press corps before turning the gun on himself . . . and missing.
- ☐ The most powerful man in the world was an orange loon with tiny hands, dodgy hair and the temperament of the spoilt little girl in *Charlie and the Chocolate Factory*.
- ☐ It doesn't matter who the President of America is, you live in Moate.

Looking to the future it's very important that we support
- ☐ Taoiseach Varadkar . . .
- ☐ Taoiseach Martin . . .
- ☐ Taoiseach Healy-Rae . . .
- ☐ Taoiseach Adams . . .

. . . when he goes to the White House on Paddy's Day delivering the traditional bowl of shamrock to President
- ☐ Trump
- ☐ Pence
- ☐ Putin
- ☐ Clinton (Chelsea)
- ☐ Kim Jong-Un

BEACH YOGA
WITH VAN MORRISON

O F ALL THE BRILLIANT TV IDEAS I've sent to RTÉ (*Hill Walking With Panti, Bring Your Daughter To Al Porter,* etc.) *Beach Yoga With Morrison* is one that the bunch of baldy beardy sandal-wearing hummus-munching clowns who run the place will live to regret passing on.

I always remember the day the nation's favourite Nordie and top funnyman rang me on the ol' 088 with this idea. I was dropping a few motts home after one of me legendary Noggin Inn sleepovers when Van's call came in. He's in me phone as 'Chuckles'.

'Heyou dooooin Dusty? Knock, Knock . . . Paddy walks into a pub . . . Why did the chicken . . . I've haaaad a great wee idea for a wee TV show . . .' Straight away he had me. 'I'm in, Van,' I said, because as one

of Ireland's greatest entreap . . . entrapmen . . . entra . . . eh . . .
as a businessman, I know a great idea even before I hear it. It's a
gift, same way that Louis Walsh knows the new Westlife album
will be brutal before the boys even get it played to them. Anyway,
Van started telling me the idea. I think he was going through a
tunnel at the time but between that, his Nordie accent and all his
laughing I still managed to get the key words: Beach, Yoga and
Speedos. I told Van to leave it with me, it'd be an easy sell and in
no time we'd be on telly and making millions with this one.

With the motts gone and Van's idea buzzing in me head I turned
the HiAce north and headed for RTÉ. To be fair to RTÉ they get a
lot of stick for being brutal at telly and radio but boy do they know
a thing or two about quality car parks. With nearly five thousand
car spaces on site in Donnybrook and most of them only used
during working hours (12.30–3pm, Tues–Thurs, Nov–Feb) it's
never hard to find a spot, so after throwing me HiAce into a prime
spot I strolled into the canteen. It was around 11am so the early
breakfast rush was in full swing. Going in the door I hid behind
Des Cahill as I needed to make sure the vultures from *The Late
Late* and *The Ray D'Arcy Show* didn't nab me. They sit by those
doors all week till they catch a line-up.

Once inside I looked for the glummest-looking soul I could find,
chances being they'd be in charge of entertainment and I could

RTÉ Car Park

start the bidding war with them for Van's new show. Wasn't hard to find the cardiganed buachaill I needed, licking a slice of toast and reading the *RTÉ Guide*. I decided to just go straight in with it. 'Boss, this is the one you've been waiting for . . . the one that will change the game for generations to come . . . this, my friend, is your *Ear to the Ground* moment.' That last one got his attention and the toast licking stopped for a few seconds. 'How would you like to be the man to land RTÉ a show that will travel the globe and make millions?' He looked me in the eye and, wiping the seven snot bubbles that were dangling from his nose, he grinned and said, 'Is maith liom.'

Then I gave him the big pitch. 'Imagine *Baywatch* only with bigger boobs, imagine *Operation Transformation* with tighter undies . . . and then, comrade, imagine *Beach Yoga with Van Morrison*.' It was then that the toast licking stopped in full as this particular Seamus sat back and said 'Dustin, agus madra fada teach aerfort ag gaire go dtí blah blah blah.' Now, I'm no gaeilgeoir but even I could tell this particular muldoon was a serious poker player; the way he managed to hide any hint of excitement or indeed any emotion whatsoever was pure class. I told him I wouldn't get into the figures there and then as clearly he was busy (again, nothing! but now I knew it was tactical) and that I'd email him the price and a few more details later.

After a pitch that went so well, you can imagine me anger when this one didn't fly. I still haven't given up on it, though, and am happy to report that TV3 are looking like its new home, though with a few tweaks as we've decided to drop the yoga and beach parts and are replacing Van with Martin King.

Probably not Van Morrison

TV WINNERS!

TELLY IS A FUNNY OLD GAME, generally made by lads who think they know what's best for everyone but who don't actually watch any telly themselves as they're simply too busy reading books (with just words) and writing scripts for movies that'll never get made. You know the type – years ago they'd have joined the church.

It's because of these lads that so many of my genius ideas for TV shows remain unmade. Some of them didn't even get to be pitched after I sent in the original written idea. And it's not just the clowns out in RTÉ who skipped on these nuggets of TV Gold but also the gang in TV3, though to be fair to them they were probably busy moving couches from *Ireland AM* to *Midday* to *Elaine* to *The Six O'Clock Show* and then out to the *Gogglebox* gaffs.

To prove to you, my dear readers, the sort of gold dust that has been thrown on the scrapheap, here's a list of some my best . . .

TATTOO NIXERS

PITCH: People get free tattoos but the twist is the tattoo artist isn't a tattoo artist and has never done a tattoo before but is willing to give it a go for €20.00 cash.

RESULT: Pitched this one to RTÉ, didn't even get a reply. So I took it to TV3, they wanted to know if we could just use 'boozed-up Irish celebrity babes abroad'.

RTÉ2

TELL THE BRIDE

PITCH: We book a private detective to dig up dirt on a groom-to-be by following him around; finishes with a honeytrap we set for him. We then doorstep the bride on the morning of the wedding with our findings for an 'emotional' end scene.

Telly Gold

RESULT: Some fool in RTÉ said they thought it was too like *Don't Tell The Bride*, where the bride cops that she's marrying an utter idiot just as he walks up the aisle.

CELEBRITY BANNISTER

PITCH: Celebrities slide down bannisters in old country manor houses.

RESULT: Marty Morrissey booked to slide down bannister at Slane Castle for RTÉ1 pilot.

3e also interested but want celebrities to be naked whilst sliding.

SHOWS WITHOUT
AL PORTER DEPT,
TV3, MARTIN KING'S
GAFF, DUBLIN

THE THORN OF TRALEE

PITCH: We find the top ten online moaners who give out endlessly about the wonderful Rose of Tralee Festival. These ten are then handcuffed to ten of last year's roses and have a month to find the handcuff keys which have been hidden somewhere in Donegal. Last to find their key has to marry the Rose they're attached to.

$$$

RESULT: Pitched to RTÉ who said they liked it but didn't know where Donegal was or if it actually existed so couldn't go with it.

NAKED BINGO

PITCH: People playing bingo in the nip.

RESULT: To be fair, this one is going to happen. TV3 have ordered 100 episodes for 3e, with Martin King presenting . . . naked.

DEADLY IDEAS UNIT,
RTÉ TELEVISION,
DONNYBROOK,
DUBLIN 4

THE BANG OF BOG
WITH A HINT OF THE
HURL FOR THOSE
WHO LIKE THE SCENT
OF SENT OFF

HEADBANGER
BY
DAVY FITZ

TOP SECRET

PIG

IN DUSTIUS WE TRUSTIUS

Ed Sheeran

Going through the leaked PIGs files, one thing is very clear: these lads are on high monitoring alert when it comes to any figure it believes may in fact be the second coming of Christ.

This 'Messiah File' is quite thick, with some surprise entries (Mikey Graham, the Rubberbandit who goes on *The Late Late* with a bag on his head, and Richie Kavanagh) along with some less surprising entries (Bono, Glen Hansard and Ronan Keating) but the most recent entry is the one that caught our eye. It makes a strong case, based on many miracles already performed, that Ed Sheeran may in fact be the second coming.

Having first come to the PIGs' attention when security at weddings around the globe was increased to stop Ed gate-crashing and turning happy couples' big days into online promos for himself, the 'Is Ed Sheeran God?' file quickly grew to become bigger than the Bible. Witnesses to one of these wedding appearances has revealed how they were traumatised when, midway through the traditional uncomfortable father-of-the-bride speech there was a small commotion as Ed turned up, took the mic and proceeded to 'sing' one of his 'songs' whilst creepily grinning at the visibly upset bride. Between her tears she was heard to ask her new husband, 'What is going on? Is this your idea of a joke? Why is Hector singing at our wedding?'

The file goes on to highlight a long list of incredible feats that suggest his powers go beyond that of normal singer-songwriters. Below is a list of Ed's more impressive miracles.

1. The Miracle of Hill 16

Ed sold out Croke Park. Ed is a ginger Brit that doesn't line-dance and Ed sold out Croke Park.

2. The Miracle of the Galway Girl

Ed has released a song called 'Galway Girl', not a cover of a song called 'Galway Girl' but instead a brand new song called 'Galway Girl'. If there's one thing the world doesn't need any more of it's songs called 'Galway Girl', yet Ed Sheeran has written, recorded and released a song called 'Galway Girl'. I've been to Galway and I've seen Galway Girls; trust me, for every Seoige there's 1,467 munters called Doireann.

A Galway Girl

3. The Miracle of the Bodhrán

Ed got bodhrán lessons and was taught how to play the bodhrán. I'm not making this up.

4. The Miracle of the Wrong Name

After vast research there is still no evidence of Ed Sheeran Sheep, despite his name.

5. The Miracle of Never Singing with Bono

UN law states that all new artists who become globally popular have to do a duet with Bono yet Ed has never sung with the Dutch rocker.

So as you can see, readers, this file presents solid evidence that simply can't be argued with. Ed Sheeran is the second coming of our Lord.

Hector tribute act Ed Sheeran looking at a camera

Ed Sheeran's Dad

Ed

Rovers Return: *Coronation Street* gets a new dog, Ken Barklow

RTÉ GUIDE DOGS

Hair of the dog: win a
Peter Barks voucher

**Fair City's new
bad boy talks
fame and peeing
in public**

**B*witched reunion
announced**

Pitbull: the
new album

Mick Woofallace:
A Dog in the Dáil

We talk to U2 frontman Bonio

FROM HEAVY METAL TO HEAVY POLITICS

WE VISIT THE WEXFORD'S TEACHTA DOG'S KENNEL

We arrived at this shaggy canine's Wexford home early and rang the bell to his beautiful kennel. The tail was wagging and we were invited in. It was Mick's first day back on the leash after the four-month Dáil recess. 'Sorry, I'm in a bit of a rush this morning. People think politics is local but for me it's national. I don't go for that parish pump thing that has ruined Ireland for so long now,' barks Mick as he sniffs our bums. With that the phone rings and his secretary Breda (a gorgeous Bichon Frise) tells Mick there's a man from Galway on the phone who says his house is about to fall off a cliff into the sea. 'I'll get back to him later,' says Mick. 'See, lads? National, not just local.'

Mick starts pawing at his hair to remove his curlers as Breda tells him yet another citizen of Ireland, this time from Cork, is on the phone to say the city is flooded and Cork now looks like Venice. 'I'll call back later,' woofs Mick.

We start the interview by asking Mick about the many different careers he's had, from builder, football manager and restaurateur to politician and guitarist with 80s heavy metal band Def Leppard.

Hole Digger

'The building started when I was a puppy. I just loved to dig in the garden, I'd spend long days just digging a hole and then filling it in again. Back then I suppose my dream job would have been with the Corpo. The football was because I always loved to chase balls – to this

'I rescued Clare Daly from a pound in Finglas'

day if anyone throws a ball near me I'll drop whatever I'm doing and run after it, though maybe leave that out or some clown in the Dáil will throw one up in the air when I'm in the middle of an important speech.'

Big Litter

'I suppose the restaurants is possibly because I'm from a litter of twelve, so once the bowls went down you just ate as quick as ya could. And of course I went into politics because I want to help people all over this great country of ours, from Dublin to Donegal and Cavan to Kerry. To me we need to look beyond just helpin' our own.'

Once again Breda enters the room with more urgent business: 57 water protesters in Dublin have just been arrested and are being sent to Guantanamo Bay. Mick says he'll deal with it in the morning.

We ask Mick about his fashion, his famous signature pink top and his golden locks. 'I never really thought about that, I've only ever had one top. Do you think anyone's ever noticed? The hair . . . I suppose that just happened by accident. I went to a groomer in Bunclody who mistook me for Twink and, hey presto – the look just suited me.'

Mick works very closely with fellow independent madra Clare Dachshund Daly and when asked tells *The Guide* about their relationship, 'Well, I rescued Clare from a pound during a protest in Fingal around 1998 and we've been allies ever since. The rest of the TDs call us The Lady and The Tramp.' He laughs briefly but then a puzzled look appears on his furry face as we ask if Clare takes offence at being called a tramp.

Mick promises to tell us about his ongoing protests at Shannon Airport against Ryanair's baggage restrictions but wants to grab a bath first. He only has time to use up three bottles of shampoo before a panicked-looking Breda enters, 'Mick! Another problem – a man from Wexford town has just been overcharged for a punnet of strawberries in Enniscorthy.' Mick jumps out of the bath buck naked as the day he was born and runs on all fours towards Enniscorthy with the speed of a Greyhound. He doesn't come back to finish our interview, but later on, *The Six One News* reports that Gardaí are warning people in the Enniscorthy area to be careful as reports have reached them that Twink has been spotted running around the town shouting 'NOT THE STRAWBERRIES! PLEASE, NO, NOT THE STRAWBERRIES!'

Def Leppard will play the Wexford Opera House as part of the Wexford Opera Festival this January.

DUSTIN GLOBAL INVE$TMENTS INC

THE NOGGIN, EUROPE

Dear Bono,

How's it goin', little man? Hope you're well and all is good in the Killiney hood!

Croker was a laugh, wasn't it? Loved the bit where ya did the ranting about Africa, was a classic . . . the face on Larry! And the bit about Trump?! Or the bit about how great the Irish are and how we all used to be Africans?! And the stuff about us being a tribe?! And the stuff about the North? Gold!

Anyways, after the billions you made from owning Facebook I was thinking you might be the type of lad with the vision to invest in my new Tech Start Up, Twatter. It's a golden one that's set to make all who throw a bit of cash my way VERY rich. It's like Twitter but with an 'A' instead of an 'I', which makes it funny sounding!

I know, I know – it's amazing no one has done this before! Also only twats will be allowed to post on it so those looking at it will know the nonsense they're reading is from certified twats and straight away they'll be able to ignore it . . . I'm hoping The Donald will be our Brand Ambassador but if he won't I'm confident I can get Nigel Farage . . . or that astrologer Russell Grant.

The get-in-early price is €20m for 7% of the company. There's only one slot left but I need to close it soon so would be willing to look at giving it to you for €19.5m in cash. A bargain I know, but hey, that's what pals are for.

Just drop it off to the usual spot and I'll get the paperwork over to you in a jiffy.

Your pal,

Dustin.

Winning Streak was originally conceived as *Winning Streaker*; the winner of the quiz would be permitted to run naked around the RTÉ campus and the general D4 area. When Marty Morrissey won the pilot the RTÉ bosses panicked knowing that a naked Marty could provoke people to return their TV licences in their millions; or worse still it could wake up some of the napping RTÉ staff. They were especially concerned when they looked at the guests for the first episode and they couldn't risk the level of sick leave a naked Twink might cause. Thus, the RTÉ boss at the time (Dr Cybil Cervice) decided to change the show and the result was the *Winning Streak* we know today, a game show that not even the presenters can understand.

Knowing the humiliation of appearing on a show like this and having to talk to

Not Marty Morrissey running

Marty Whelan, RTÉ duped the lottery into paying for the show so contestants could be guaranteed hard cash and a car that they could sell on Done Deal straight away.

WATCHING WINNING STREAK

NOT *WATCHING* WINNING STREAK

PRESENTERS

In 1990 Mike Murphy was first up to present this heap of manure, but after shouting 'It's Waterford again!' and 'It's Cork again!' for a decade, he was replaced in 2000 by Derek Mooney who made it his own by shouting 'It's Mayo again!' and 'It's Carlow again!' until 2008 when he was replaced by Aidan Power and Carlow Protestant Kathryn Thomas. The duo didn't work, though it did start well when RTÉ decided on a radical approach by putting out the first episode in the wrong order, opening with Part 3 and closing with Part 2, a move that went largely unnoticed by the viewing audience. Things weren't helped by a suited Aidan looking like he was making his confo each week. Kathryn was sent by RTÉ to *Operation Transformation*, though personally I think she is the perfect weight and would suggest if they want to increase the ratings they bring her and the original 'streaker' concept back straight away.

By 2010 RTÉ were desperate to get rid of it but knew if they just axed it the nutters would be on to *Liveline* in their thousands so they hatched a plan to kill it with kindness by digging up Marty Whelan and getting him shouting 'It's Limerick again!', 'It's Laois again!' and 'It's Donegal again!'. To RTÉ's shock moustachioed Marty made the show more popular than ever by ingeniously adding an extra county to his shout-outs, in the process winning the hearts of boggers all over Ireland.

But the truth is, it's not down to Mike, Derek, Kathryn, Aidan or Marty. The real stars of *Winning Streak* aren't even the contestants; the real stars are the audience members. Sitting there each week with faces that show equal measures of fear and excitement, these people generally look like they may have just escaped from somewhere for the day. This is because generally many of these people have just escaped from somewhere for the day – typically it's some town in the Midlands but it's always somewhere outside Dublin. God love them but the combination of seeing 'inside the tellybox' and having their wife/cousin win some cash leaves them in such a state of confusion that they often wave at monitors and ask Marty Whelan for a selfie – this is especially worrying as none of them have smartphones.

Winning Streak is now Europe's longest running game show but as Ireland is Europe's longest running sitcom this is no huge surprise. Like the bad weather, taxes and Linda Martin, *Winning Streak* will be with us forever, not least of all because all boggers love to scratch.

Marty Whelan, Moustachioed King of Selfies

SMELL ANGRY & *Glam*
AT THE SAME TIME

BY

PANTI

Dundalk

PLAYING THE HARP, DEFENDING THE HARP, DRINKING THE HARP

LOCATION
This kip is in County Louth, which is most famous for not being Meath and is also known as 'The Wee County', due to the smell of urine that wafts across it. It's just south of the border with Nordieland, as The Brits took one look at the place and said we could hold on to it.

HISTORY
The Dundalk area has been inhabited since 3500 BC and to be honest not much has changed since then. The Normans arrived in 1169 but decided any damage they would do to the town would only improve it. Dundalk has a strong association with Setanta who later changed his name to Cu Chulainn because he didn't want to be named after a sports channel. The town's

motto is 'Mé do rug Cu Chulainn Croga' ('I gave birth to brave Cu Chulainn') mainly said by the womenfolk to claim money on child allowance day. Dundalk's most famous 'THING' is a rock where legend has it the mythological hero tied himself standing up rather than fall in battle, proving he was stupid enough to live here.

ACCENT
Close your eyes and think of the sound a Cavan lad would make if he was trying to sound even thicker than he actually is, then slow it down, add a Nordie twang and imagine a sentence never, never being completed.

HONOURS/LOCALS OF NOTE
Gerry Adams has topped the poll in the last two elections here, winning The Dundalk Rose crown, but sadly he has failed both

Dundalk St Patrick's Day Parade 2017

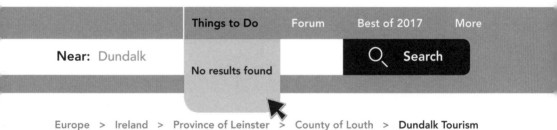

Things to Do   Forum   Best of 2017   More

Near: Dundalk

No results found

🔍 **Search**

Europe > Ireland > Province of Leinster > County of Louth > **Dundalk Tourism**

Franchise opportunities exist, apply now to Dundalk Enterprise

times to make it through to the televised stages of The Rose Of Tralee.

Dundalk decided to cash in on its 'Rock and Roll' residents after seeing how well it worked for Dalkey. However, it never really took off as by then local musician Jim Corr had moved to Jupiter so he could be closer to Flash Gordon; and local band Bagatelle (whose biggest hit 'Summer in Dublin' was about the joys of not being in Dundalk) were on the official Missing People's Register.

Dundalk Institute of Technology opened in 1970. Courses include:

1. Dog grooming and watching *Emmerdale*
2. Accounting (sorry, just counting)
3. English (learning to speak it)
4. Knitting (balaclavas)
5. How to use Aertel (four-year diploma)
6. Spieling

7. Taking selfies
8. How to book a Ryanair flight (UK and Ireland only)
9. More knitting
10. Emigration/ballad singing

LOCAL ENTERPRISE

In 2006 Dundalk Ice Dome opened. Set up to become 'a centre of excellence for ice hockey in Ireland' (I am not making this up) it closed in 2010 with the loss of 19 jobs and 49 ice skates.

Plans to reopen and stage 'We'll Meat Again – The Larry Goodman Musical on Ice' about the trials (many) and tribulations (not so many) of the local beef baron stalled as Disney have pulled their investment.

This is NOT photoshopped. This IS a sign in Dundalk

TWINNED
Pikeville, Kentucky (do yer own jokes).

POPULATION
Who's asking?

PASTIMES AND HOBBIES
The Harp.

PROVINCE
Who's asking?

Dundalk: The Land of One Welcome

As part of the Good Friday Agreement the Brits were finally allowed into Dundalk

An office that Gerry Adams has 'never been in', 'never seen', 'never passed' and doesn't even know exists

DIALING CODE
088.

VISITOR GUIDE
Who's asking?

CULTURE
Sting holidays in the town and wrote the song 'An Englishman in Dundalk' but due to lack of international airplay and poor chart positioning changed it to 'Englishman in New York'.

COMMENTS

Search

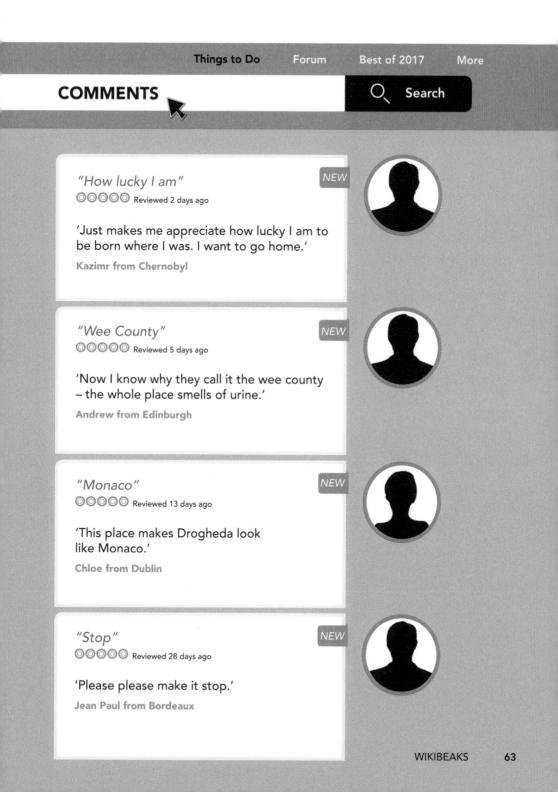

"How lucky I am"
NEW
◎◎◎◎◎ Reviewed 2 days ago

'Just makes me appreciate how lucky I am to be born where I was. I want to go home.'

Kazimr from Chernobyl

"Wee County"
NEW
◎◎◎◎◎ Reviewed 5 days ago

'Now I know why they call it the wee county – the whole place smells of urine.'

Andrew from Edinburgh

"Monaco"
NEW
◎◎◎◎◎ Reviewed 13 days ago

'This place makes Drogheda look like Monaco.'

Chloe from Dublin

"Stop"
NEW
◎◎◎◎◎ Reviewed 28 days ago

'Please please make it stop.'

Jean Paul from Bordeaux

How to hit a hipster
(where it hurts)

Are you a hipster?

If you're reading this book, chances are you're probably not a hipster – unless you're reading the Penguin Classic edition or listening to the audio on vinyl. But if in fact you are a hipster, I have some good news: there is now a cure, based on the ancient Chinese medicine known as 馄饨汤, which translates as 'cop yourself on and stop being a tool – you're from Navan'.

While large parts of the world have emerged blinking from behind their Ray-Bans on the other side of the hipster epidemic, there are sadly still large pockets of hipsterdom in Ireland. Legally you are not allowed to hit a hipster. This is a good thing as hitting is usually frowned upon in our modern liberal society.* However, it's been medically proven that the urge to slap a passing hipster is so strong that many simply can't resist. With this in mind, I've drawn up these well-researched guidelines on how to avoid/annoy hipsters:

1. Stay away from Stoneybatter.
2. Avoid any music festival that thinks it's 'a picnic' or has a spoken word section. This is also good general life advice.
3. Instead of hitting them physically (a bad thing) there are other ways to hit them where it hurts:
     - Tamper with the bells on their bicycles
     - Reduce their bloodflow by putting shrinking powder in the wash with their skinny jeans
     - Add itching powder to their beard wax
     - Place dingleberries in their organic soya-infused coffee
     - Pour actual jam into their jam jars
     - Insinuate melody into their music.
4. Avoid anywhere that serves food on slates, bricks, table tennis bats or old *Beano* annuals.

For hints on how to hit a liberal, see next year's 'not so funny' volume two of this book.

5. Whisper 'You are a sheep' to them repeatedly when they are asleep.
6. Show the bearded ones photos of Yanks with mullets and ask if they're related.
7. Offer them 'a job'.
8. Call cupcakes 'buns'.
9. Invite a few around to your pad to watch a silent movie made in Russia in the 1920s, then bang on a DVD of *Fast and Furious 7*.
10. Ask them if all actors are allowed to wear their stage clothes out and about.

There ya go; do all that and pretty soon these clowns will be a thing of the past . . . just like vinyl.

EUROVISION SONG CONTEST

I'm a Vision! No! Eurovision!

I knew my world had gone a bit weird when, backstage at the Eurovision '08 in Belgrade, two blokes painted blue with no tops on and cones for heads walked past me and the only thing that looked odd to me was that they weren't holding hands.

So, how did I get there?

I remember well the moment RTÉ first begged me to take part in Eurovision. It was exactly three minutes after Dervish had lost the thing with a song written by the Chuckle-Brother-in-Chief, John Waters. I was in me nest when the mobile went and an RTÉ head (who shall remain clueless) was on the line. He got straight to the begging, telling me I was the only one that could do it for Ireland, the only one with the talent and looks that could get us back to where we belonged. He said it wasn't just my duty but also an opportunity for me to bring my genius to a global audience.

I asked 'How much?'

We agreed a cash-only deal* there and then and the rest is history.

There was a national outrage, questions were asked in the Dáil, CNN were covering the story and *The New York Times* got in touch too. Some lad in Cork even did a thesis on my song's effect on Ireland's relationship with Europe. (I am not making this up.)

Punters often ask me what the Eurovision is actually like and I tell them it's like stepping into an episode of *My Little Pony*, where the flying pink pony appears normal beside the likes of Dana and Johnny Logan and various other sufferers of PEDD (Post Eurovision Delusion Disorder). It's a cruel disorder with symptoms that can see some former winners believe they should be president while others permanently dress like it's 1986 and at all times insist on carrying a guitar they don't know how to play.

For reasons of national security I'm not allowed to reveal the details of this deal. Put it this way: I'm not surprised they sold their back field this year.

EURO♥ISION
SONG CONTEST

It's a ridiculous competition that costs millions and has produced more brutal songs than Westlife and Boyzone combined. Its audience is like a cross between a Right Said Fred reunion concert and the audience from *Winning Streak*. And for these reasons alone it must continue forever. We need more things like the Eurovision in this insane world – things people care about so much but are at the same time completely useless.

Five minutes after those two blue lads walked by me I was in a shopping trolley robbed from a Tesco in Ballyfermot and belting out one of the greatest songs ever written to an audience of gazillions around the world. As some of you more tuned-in readers may be aware, there were some technical issues that night that resulted in billions of votes for me not being registered. I could have made a big deal of it, I could have gone legal and won billions in damages but I'm a peace-lovin' bird and, as John Lennon used to say, 'Koo Koo Cachoo' . . . or 'let it be', or something like that.

Either way Eurovision is the best craic you'll ever have and that's why I'm delighted to announce here in *WikiBeaks* that I'm going to enter again for he 2018 contest in Portugal. I've not decided which country. Turkey has made an offer but I'm also in talks with the Brits about doing a duet with Basil Brush. Failing that I am also in talks to put together a cross-border super-group made up of Dana, Panti, Arlene Foster, Julian from UTV and Judge from *Wanderly Wagon*.

You wou[...]
these tw[...]

Below are ten Euro Facts; one of them isn't true. Can you guess which one is the Sean Spicer?

1. Dana drinks pints of blood before every gig.
2. Linda Martin was 93 when she won with 'Why Me?'
3. Johnny Logan is Latin for 'Perfectly sane, no chip on no shoulder here, boss'.
4. The Pope has attended three Eurovisions dressed in disguise as The Pope. No one spotted him.
5. 'My Lovely Horse' is not about Linda Martin.
6. Brexit could see the UK delegation become even more unpopular with the other nations, though many believe that's actually impossible.
7. Roy Keane has written the Croatian entry every year for the last five years.
8. Every year Dana's moustache has its own fan club event at Eurovision.
9. Marty Whelan had lucky Eurovision underpants. Ireland haven't won the Eurovision in 22 years. Marty needs new jocks.
10. If you play 'The Voice' by Eimear Quinn backwards it sounds exactly the same.

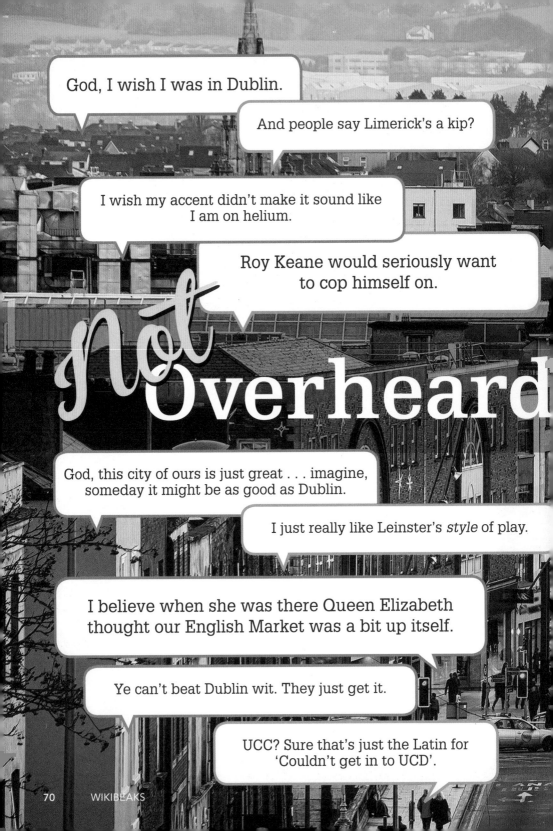

God, I wish I was in Dublin.

And people say Limerick's a kip?

I wish my accent didn't make it sound like I am on helium.

Roy Keane would seriously want to cop himself on.

Not Overheard

God, this city of ours is just great . . . imagine, someday it might be as good as Dublin.

I just really like Leinster's *style* of play.

I believe when she was there Queen Elizabeth thought our English Market was a bit up itself.

Ye can't beat Dublin wit. They just get it.

UCC? Sure that's just the Latin for 'Couldn't get in to UCD'.

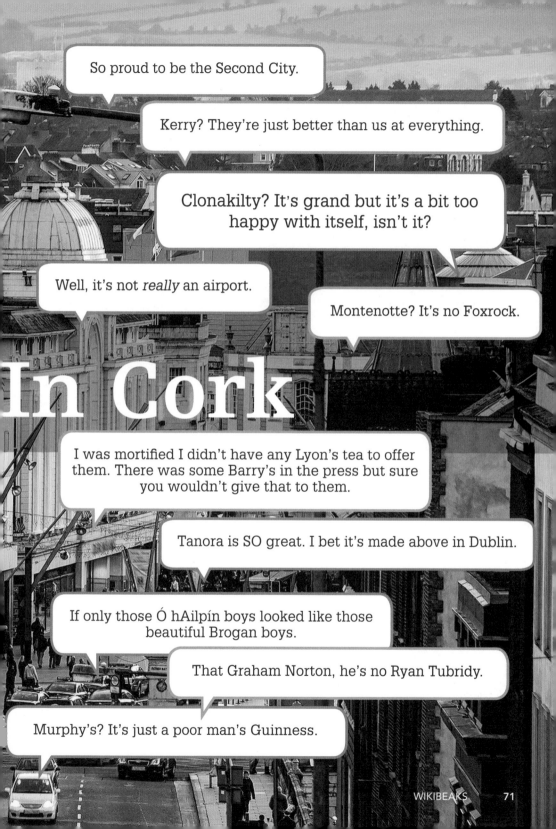

So proud to be the Second City.

Kerry? They're just better than us at everything.

Clonakilty? It's grand but it's a bit too happy with itself, isn't it?

Well, it's not *really* an airport.

Montenotte? It's no Foxrock.

In Cork

I was mortified I didn't have any Lyon's tea to offer them. There was some Barry's in the press but sure you wouldn't give that to them.

Tanora is SO great. I bet it's made above in Dublin.

If only those Ó hAilpín boys looked like those beautiful Brogan boys.

That Graham Norton, he's no Ryan Tubridy.

Murphy's? It's just a poor man's Guinness.

There are some people out there who think I, one of Ireland's greatest ever musical artists, am guilty of crimes against music. These people are not well in the head and clearly have hearing issues. I will admit I'm not proud of the time I brought Bob Geldof with me to the top of the charts, a regret I'll take with me to my grave, along with the regret I have about the time I bet Ray D'Arcy his show couldn't be duller than the one Brendan O'Connor used to do. You can say what you like about Ray but he doesn't like to lose a bet.

But if my musical output is criminal, *X Factor* is a death row where songs go to spend their last days before being murdered live on TV in front of a line-up of judges whose faces now have officially more plastic in them than your average Lego man.

Back when it first started it was good craic but ever since Simon Cowell stopped wearing his trousers at neck level something has gone seriously wrong. For the last few years *X Factor* has been on a trolley in A&E, lying there in the hope that someone will decide to look at it and make it feel better. You know a show is in deep, deep trouble when the solution to its problems is to rehire Louis Walsh. Ronan Keating can't half-fill Whelan's these days and even he hasn't rehired Louis Walsh.

But to be fair to Louis he's still the best thing on the show. The joker in the pack, you sit there hoping he'll deliver a classic

You remind me of a young Jackie Chan.

line or two, and week in, week out, he doesn't let you down. It's not always up there with the time he told Rowetta, the R'n'B singer from Manchester, that she reminded him of 'a young Jackie Chan' (I'm not making this up) but it is always great.

No, for me the problem is Simon Cowell. It's clear that Simon loves music. Having first fallen in love with music as a young child he has spent his life trying to show the rest of the world just how amazing he believes music is.

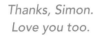

You know what? I love you, Simon.

Thanks, Simon. Love you too.

Programme. As soon as you leave the stage covered in glitter, you disappear and are never heard of again. It's like picking the winning Lotto numbers, throwing a huge party to celebrate and then putting your best suit in the wash for the cheque presentation . . . and leaving the winning ticket in the pocket.

In order to help fix this once great show I've come up with a three-point plan:

1. Anyone who says it's 'their dream' or that they want to 'win it for their Grandad' will automatically be sent to prison for ten years with no chance of parole.

2. The judges' chairs will be electric and viewers will be able to issue shocks every time Louis Walsh compares an auditionee to somebody actually talented; whenever Cowell says 'You know what?'; if any judge 'cries'; or whenever Sharon Osbourne or Nicole Whatsherface fart.

3. A year after they win, the winning act gets to give Cowell a wedgy live on The News if they don't end up having a career.

(Oh wait . . . hang on, sorry. I just re-read that last paragraph and there've been a few huge typos. Please see the correct version below . . .)

No, for me the problem is Simon Cowell. It's clear that Simon loves Simon. Having first fallen in love with Simon as a young child Simon has spent his life trying to show the rest of the world just how amazing Simon believes Simon is.

Winning *X Factor* these days is like being put into the Witness Protection

These three simple steps will without fail restore this once great show to its rightful place at the top of the TV tree.

Now, who do I invoice for this advice? Cash only.

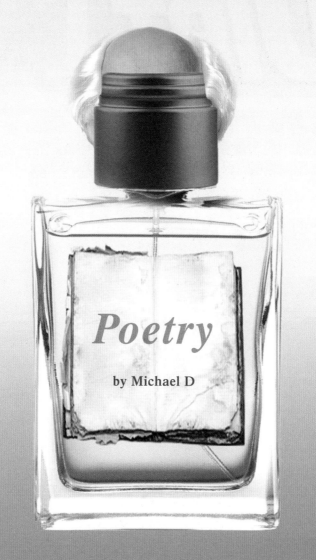

THE WHIFF OF THE WESHT

Poetry

by Michael D

Because EVERY Occasion Needs a Poem

THE DAILY DIRT

10c

ROSANNA DAVISON

CLINGY!

BUT . . . ROSIE IS THE ONE WITH THE SWEETEST-SMELLING FARTS

'I'D RATHER BE AN OUTLAW THAN AN IN-LAW,' SAYS DUSTIN

I know, I know: I still can't believe she was half made by pint-sized monobrow musical maestro Chris de Burgh but when it comes to kissing she'd be in my Top 100. Of all the Miss Worlds I've kissed she's second only to Miss Isle of Man.

For a lot of lads Rosie is dream wife material, but that's before they consider the in-law implications, which for me were a step too far. What me and herself had was special, and I know she saw me as the man she would spend the rest of her life with but after just one Sunday lunch with her old lad prattling on and threatening to play me some 'new material' I just had to leg it. No mott is worth that.

I'll admit there's times I do miss Rosie and I'll tell you one thing – of all the motts I've been with, Rosie is the one with the sweetest-smelling farts. They're almost lavender-like. She said it was because she was a vegan but I really don't think I was her first.

> Of all the motts I've been with, Rosie is the one with the sweetest-smelling farts.

The media made a lot of fuss about me not attending the wedding but the simple truth is I'd a bingo night on in the pigeon club and I wish her and the doctor's son all the happiness in the world . . . and, Wes, you're NOT a rebound; she only calls me twice a day.

MAD VERTS

MY REVOLUTIONARY TRUTH-BASED AD AGENCY

Nations often strive for greatness, setting incredible goals to aspire to. Great nations like America, China, Russia and Luxembourg triumph in sport, the arts, science and salad dressing because they look at the world in a certain way. They see things that appear impossible and they go all out to conquer them.

In Ireland we see things differently. While greatness is a good thing, we prefer to celebrate those who ALMOST achieve it. We have parades for teams that lose quarter-finals; we consider bronze to be better than gold when one of ours brings it home; and we think *Room To Improve* is must-see TV.

Almost Nationwide . . .

One crowd who've turned 'Almost' into a secret weapon are Shaw's Department Stores. By declaring this with their famous 'Almost Nationwide' slogan, they've become the envy of the retail world with Harrods, Macy's and Saks Fifth Avenue all sending spies out to Athy and Dun Laoghaire to see just how Shaw's manage to create their unique shopping experience, which has seen customers travel for miles to double park outside and spend their dole on Clarks shoes and Wranglers.

This genius stroke of marketing honesty got me thinking that there might be a buck to be made by pitching a similar approach to a bunch of other businesses. I'm calling these Dustin's mADVERTS because you'd be mad not to like 'em. I predict I will become the biggest ad agency in the world over the next six months. Almost . . .

Supermac's – Almost Edible

Eddie Rocket's – Almost Affordable

Tesco Express – Getting Your Money to Britain Every Hour on the Hour

Irish Rail – All Track and No Craic

AIB – We're Backing Gullible

Ryanair – We Don't Care

Volkswagen – Emissions? Impossible!

Pepsi – Sorry, We're out of Coke

The Abbey Theatre – Supporting Dead Writers with Your Cash

Jury's Inn – €260.00 for a bed beside Croker? The Jury's out!

Guinness – Turning Your Arse into James's Gate

Penney's – First-hand clothes at second-hand prices, made by third-world hands

IKEA – Where a Good Healthy Marriage Can End in an Hour

And then Dustin said we'd only make ads that told the truth!

Louis Vuitton – No, we're not taking the piss . . .

KFC – Knot Feckin' Chicken

RTÉ2 – Move Along Now, There's Nothing to See Here

2FM – Where Even Great Songs Sound Brutal

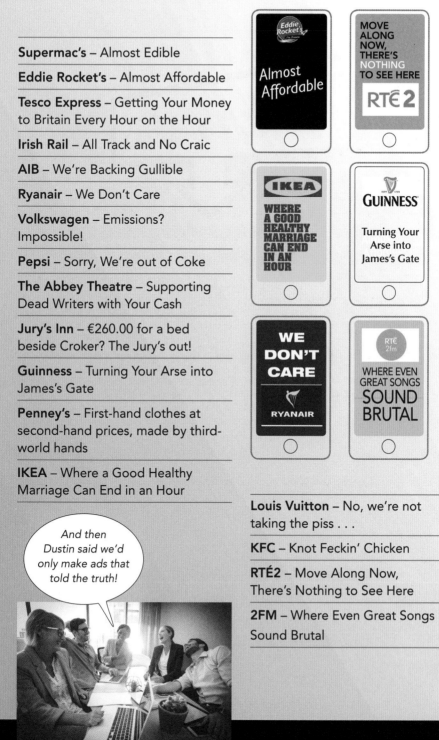

Almost Affordable

MOVE ALONG NOW, THERE'S NOTHING TO SEE HERE
RTÉ 2

IKEA
WHERE A GOOD HEALTHY MARRIAGE CAN END IN AN HOUR

GUINNESS
Turning Your Arse into James's Gate

WE DON'T CARE
RYANAIR

RTÉ 2fm
WHERE EVEN GREAT SONGS SOUND BRUTAL

TOP TEN SPOOFERS

Some nations produce great athletes, some nations produce great artists but here in Ireland we can lay claim to being the home to more spoofers per square mile than any other country on earth. To honour these great men and women I have writ a list of me fave top ten chancers in chief . . .

1 Bertie Ahern
The only Minister for Finance who didn't have a bank account apart from The Right Honourable Abdul Hakmhed O'Malley of Sierra Leone.

2 Louis Walsh
A bogger lad who can't even clap properly and yet manages to make millions out of judging talent – now THAT'S quality spoofing.

3 Michael O'Leary
In any other country this lad wouldn't be allowed to run a tap. Here people trust him with their lives . . .

4 Keith Duffy
Can't sing, can't dance, can't act, can't believe his luck.

Bill Cullen

On the plus side this former *Apprentice* 'star' is too thick to have run for president but you have to hand it to a bloke that can be a used car salesman and convince people he's a genius at the same time, his buuk *From Penny Apples* is basically *The Spoofer's Guide To Spoofing*. Should be on the Leaving Cert.

The Red Squirrel

A nut-hoarding rat with a tail, this lad is the Irish animal world's version of Joan Burton – friendly but vicious.

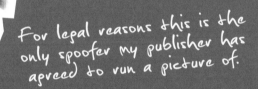

For legal reasons this is the only spoofer my publisher has agreed to run a picture of.

Philip Boucher-Hayes

He uses three names and a posh voice to con people into thinking he's clever. I've met smarter pigeons.

Sr Stan

Claims to be a sister but is called Stan. 'Nuff said.

Patrick Bergin

Dick from *Glenroe*'s brother, this genius spoofer has managed to turn once appearing as 'man in shop' in a Julia Roberts film into a career.

Denis O'Brien

As my lawyer just told me Denis O'Brien is a man of impeccable standing with zero faults and whilst he's very definitely not a spoofer, if he was a spoofer he'd definitely be number one on this list, sitting on top of Bertie Ahern.

#Repealthe8th

Politics can be a lonely oul' trade. You can spend years banging on about an issue and feel no one is really listening. But if you believe strongly enough it's pretty much impossible to stop sharing your passion for it.

But sometimes, something amazing, something totally unpredictable happens and it restores your faith, not only in politics but in humanity too.

As you all know I've got certain views of Culchies. I don't hate them and I'd never suggest a Culchie Cull or anything like that. Ever. The truth is, I'm actually very fond of Culchies, I've been known from time to time to listen to The Saw Doctors, and while I draw the line at Bon Jovi and Nathan Carter, I have listened to Meat Loaf at weddings (the church part) after a Rock Shandy or two. No, my mission with Culchies has always been simply to kind of fix them through conversion therapy, bring them into the modern world of cars, electricity and marrying outside your own, and to generally help them become as smart, cultured and handsome as your average Dub. Unlikely I know, but we must dare to dream. As Martin King says, 'I have a dream.' Well, so do I, Martin, so do I and unlike yours, mine doesn't feature Lucy Kennedy.

ofDecember

I dream of a world where Culchies can have all the things we have in Dublin in their own gaffs, villages, towns and caravans. That they too can visit Dr Quirkey if they're feeling down. That they too can have proper chippers, dinners in the evening, new clothes that aren't just from concerts in Slane, smartphones and not just phone boxes, meals without coleslaw and more channels than just RTÉ1 and RTÉ1+1. I want them to be educated enough that they won't be afraid of The Luas when they come up to Croker.

Part of my campaign is to encourage them to stay and spend their hard-farmed money in their own shops. They'll never evolve if they keep just coming up to my beautiful city every time there's a sale on. Some people have described my call for a complete and immediate ban on all Culchies coming into Dublin as racist. It's not; Culchies aren't a race. But as a seasoned politician, I know I need to listen to the people, so a few years ago I proposed a symbolic ban, one that makes my point and highlights the need for Culchies to stay where they are in Culchie-land.

As you all know, December the 8th is traditionally the day that Culchies descend on my Dublin to do their Christmas shopping. They gather early at Clery's Clock and they spread across the city in groups, targeting Guiney's in the morning (no one's told them it's gone) eating a full carvery dinner at 11am and then drinking 'til Copper's opens. Well, I decided a few years ago that my beautiful city won't stand for this annual invasion anymore, so I set up a campaign to Repeal the Annual 8th of December Culchie Invasion, under the catchier banner of Repeal The 8th.

AND THE WORD IS, THEY DON'T WANT US UP ABOVE IN DUBLIN ON THE 8TH

Main Mayo to Dublin road

I don't mind admitting that the first few years of the campaign were quiet enough but then, out of the blue over the last year, the public have embraced the idea with the kind of passion I've not seen since that night Ray D'Arcy had Shirley Temple Bar up to his place for dinner. It's incredible, everywhere I go I see happy smiley young people wearing my Repeal message on their clothes.

Grafton Street, last 8 December (lunchtime)

Now, when I say happy and smiley faces it's fair to say one or two of these Grainnes, Aoifes and Fiachras could do with a tickle* or two. But that's just because they believe ridding Dublin of Culchies is a serious, serious matter and they are serious, serious people, who I'm proud to say are willing to stand up for their serious, serious beliefs. Thanks to them, I feel Dublin is only years off its first Culchie-Free Dec 8th.

Repeal The 8th!

*Though I wouldn't recommend tickling them personally. Trust me, they don't like it.

DECEMBER

8

Win an iBone 7

RTÉGUIDEDOGS

Dig your own hole

Don't Tell the Bride

Miriam O'Colliechan: Bark for the Park

The Greyhound Diet: We talk to Sonia O'Sullivan

'I won't hit any more Paddies':
Jeremy Barkson on his Shock Return to *Top Gear*

The Great Irish Bark-off: We go behind the scenes

IS MIRIAM SNIFFING THE ÁRAS?
WE FIND OUT...

It's a busy Miriam O'Colliechan who greets us outside her kennel. Oozing her legendary sincerity, she offers us a bowl of water and a Bonio. Miriam loves a Bonio.

It's all go as the mum of 487, all of them bouncing around happily, explains that she's about to put it on the market after spotting a great new gaff in the Phoenix Park. 'The pups are getting to that age where we just need more space to bring their pals around; 1,476 of them were here last week for Fifi's debs. The poor young pup that was her date was so excited I had to put a lead on him,

did an ice bucket challenge before presenting *Prime Time*; and shortly after the show came off air she found herself holding up a giant cardboard iPhone with Sonia O'Sullivan on Grafton Street for the launch of The Give A Dog A Phone campaign. Miriam is an Ambassador for the campaign which she proudly tells us brings her number of ambassadorships to 548, though she's quick to point out that she doesn't accept every ambassadorship, having only last week turned down an offer to be the face of National Worming Week.

> *'It's no secret I love dressing up. I'd have a new collar and lead every day if I could'*

take him for a walk and then throw a bucket of water over him to calm him down. Also, once I get the gaff in the park I will be able to work from home.'

Amazingly, Miriam still manages to find the time to tweet about her incredible and endless charity work. Unafraid to get stuck in at the frontline, the night before we met, Miriam had attended six charity balls, run four mini marathons and

No conversation with Miriam is complete without bringing up 'those park rumours'. At first she goes all coy, saying there's no point in talking about it, but of course she's flattered. It's surprising to hear a woman of her obvious elegance claim to be flattered about rumours that she was seen sniffing around the Pooper Scooper bin in Bushy Park, but who are we to judge this clearly formidable dog?

Bath-time is busy-time in Miriam's kennel

Discussing her future plans Miriam tells us that her top priority is always her family. This year she will be fronting an eight-part series on parenting where she has agreed to accept a challenge to attempt to remember all her kids' names. Her chat show will also be back, and Miriam is buoyant about it: 'I've just found out that Sonia has been confirmed for every episode!' There were initial concerns that the Cork greyhound might only be available for nine of the ten episodes this year.

A stickler for detail, Miriam is already working on her wardrobe. 'It's no secret that I love dressing up in fab dresses but this year I think I've really nailed it. I met a gorgeous woman called Panti Bliss at a charity lunch and, honestly, from the moment I laid eyes on her I knew I had found my look. The best thing is that Panti is lending me all her fab dresses, so viewers can expect the style on this year's series to be off the charts!'

Time spent with Miriam is always fun. After a good four hours she stops talking long enough for us to say it is time for us to go. Ever the gracious host, she shows us out and tells us with a wink that the next time she will get her Aide-de-camp to drop us home. We have no idea what she means so we just wink back, sniff her bum and say our goodbyes.

PIG

IN DUSTIUS WE TRUSTIUS

CLASSIFIED

PIGs FILE THREE

NELSON MANDELA

The PIGs file on Nelson Mandela is a small one and the PIGs agents may have been drunk when they wrote it as there is zero mention of the column built in his honour on O'Connell Street.

Nelson Mandela spent 27 years in prison, 18 of them in an 8 x 7ft cell on Robben Island, though for legal reasons I need to point out that he wasn't in Robben for robbing. Daft.ie believe that if the cell was in Dublin it could now fetch €1.2 million.

Once out of prison Nelson Mandela often spoke of his many connections to Ireland. During the Northern Ireland peace talks he was frequently asked to counsel the various participants on how best to deal with Bono, a move that many credit with saving Bono's life. Reports that Bertie Ahern used to get the giggles at Nelson's accent have never been 100% confirmed.

On his many trips to Dublin he was often spotted in Champion Sports picking out new shiny purple tracksuits and outside Bruxelles chatting to the Phil Lynott statue about what he's been up to since he got out of Shawshank.

In his later years he received more than 250 honours which is a great Leaving Cert in anyone's book. The Royal College of Surgeons made him a Fellow, which was thoughtful of them but there's no record of him ever picking him up. As he had used rugby to help heal ancient divides in South Africa, the GAA asked him how they might use their games to stop people fighting here. He watched a hurling match and afterwards asked if he was on *Candid Camera*.

After leaving prison Nelson never reoffended and went on to meet The Spice Girls.

kipAdvisor®

Portlaoise

NOWHERE NEAR A PORT

Another kip our Government does not want us to know about is Portlaoise, situated in the Midlands – or as it's known to the few people who have visited it, the Midblands.

The town was founded in 1987 by Mary Kennedy and Michael Ryan while shooting a *Nationwide* special on people who make jam. I was eager to see how bad things are there for myself, but after an hour on a train from Dublin, we pulled into Portlaoise station to find that the last two carriages had been robbed and melted down for metal parts (or jewellery, as it's known around here). During my visit I learned a lot of interesting facts:

- The prison in the centre of the town is known to the locals as 'Trinity' as it's only the really smart townsfolk that get in.
- This place is as dull as it is flat; a Friday night out here has all the excitement of a Coldplay concert.
- When Oliver Cromwell said to the people of Portlaoise 'to Hell or to Connacht', locals thought they were being offered a choice of two holidays.
- In 2014, in an attempt to prove they actually have a sense of humour, Kim Kardashian and Kanye West famously honeymooned here. Reports say that for the first three days they actually thought they were visiting a famine theme park. Kanye decided to treat Kim to a night at the local cinema but the movie had to be cancelled when the piano player didn't turn up.
- Every year African schoolkids are given Trócaire boxes with images of Portlaoise natives on them. Bob Geldof has frequently been asked by African friends to do another LIVE AID for the town.
- Every September the menfolk of the town head to nearby Stradbally to look at people who don't have six fingers and three eyes going to something called the EP.
- During the boom, many Dubliners were forced to move here, at first locals did not want them on 'their turf', but are now thankful that the Dubs introduced them

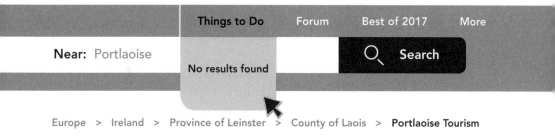

| | Things to Do | Forum | Best of 2017 | More |

Near: Portlaoise

No results found

🔍 **Search**

Europe > Ireland > Province of Leinster > County of Laois > **Portlaoise Tourism**

to the indoor toilet, toothpaste and sliced pan bread.

- Famous Irish *Love/Hate* actor and heartthrob Robert Sheehan (who I often get mistaken for) hails from the town. Oddly enough he's since chosen to live elsewhere.

After discovering the 'charm' of the town I went to get the train back, but the locals had beaten me to it and eaten the last remaining carriages. So the bus it was. On the bus back I met Meta from Copenhagen, who told me she had cut her holiday to Ireland by two weeks and had booked a

Kim and Kanye were here. No, really, they were . . .

Ryanair flight back to Denmark for €8,645. I tried to tell her that not all of Ireland was like Portlaoise. But when I saw from her itinerary that her next port of call was gonna be Tullamore I told the bus driver to hurry up.

POPULATION
22,050.

POPULATION ON REMAND
22,014.

MOTTO
'Portlaoise: Home Of The Portaloo'.

The Trinity College of the Midlands

kipAdvisor®

Portlaoise | **Hotels** ▼ | Holiday Rentals | Restaurants

Find:
Cell Block A
Cell Block B
Cell Block C

Top Bunk
Bottom Bunk
Solitary Confinement

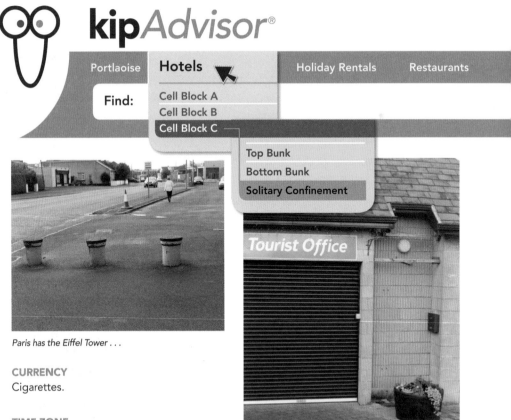

Paris has the Eiffel Tower . . .

Portlaoise's Botanic Gardens

CURRENCY
Cigarettes.

TIME ZONE
Late 1950s.

CLIMATE
Miserable.

LANGUAGE
Polish.

EIRCODE
DuMP 487.

DENSITY
Yes. (Very.)

NOTABLE RESIDENTS
Sean O'Rourke, Bartholomew Mosse and Robert Sheehan. (That's right: THE Bartholomew Mosse.)

Portlaoise's Banksy

COMMENTS

🔍 Search

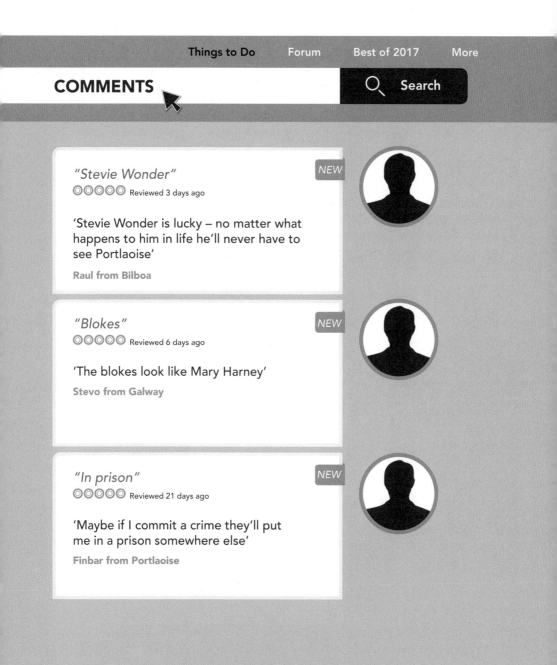

"Stevie Wonder"
ⓒⓒⓒⓒⓒ Reviewed 3 days ago   NEW

'Stevie Wonder is lucky – no matter what happens to him in life he'll never have to see Portlaoise'

Raul from Bilboa

"Blokes"
ⓒⓒⓒⓒⓒ Reviewed 6 days ago   NEW

'The blokes look like Mary Harney'

Stevo from Galway

"In prison"
ⓒⓒⓒⓒⓒ Reviewed 21 days ago   NEW

'Maybe if I commit a crime they'll put me in a prison somewhere else'

Finbar from Portlaoise

Dermot Bannon
Does the Famine...

Few people know that Dermot Bannon was around during the famine, or 'The Great Famine' as he called it, proving the lad was destined to work in property all along. Much like Dermot himself, the famine wasn't much craic, but can you imagine the agony of starving to death and then getting a visit from Dermot and his crew to discuss what improvements he'd make to your hovel? You'd be telling him you wanted some food or you'd die and he'd be staring up at your ceiling telling you what you really needed was some more natural light. You'd beg him for a feed and he'd convince you that a glass-box extension would be the solution to all your woes. It's really no wonder millions chose the coffin ships.

Here at WikiBeaks HQ we've discovered pictures that show the impact TV's greatest spoofer had on the Irish landscape during its most troubled era.

I'LL NEVER GET ON THE JOHN HINDE
POSTCARD NOW

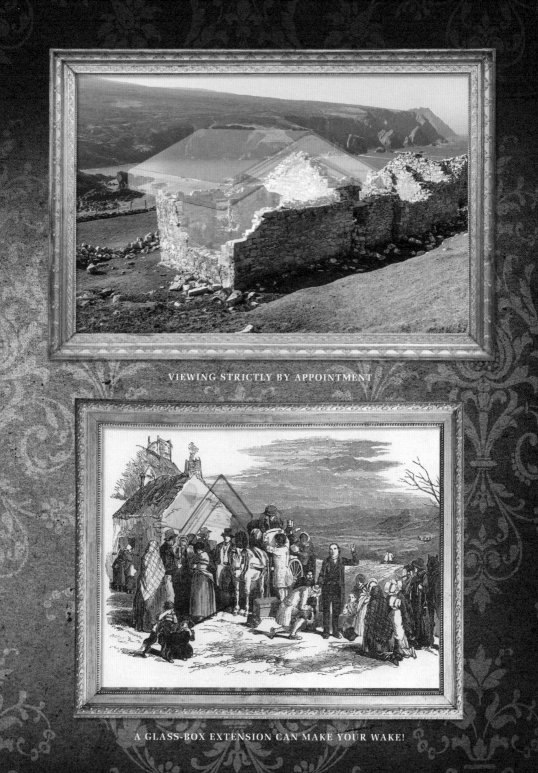

VIEWING STRICTLY BY APPOINTMENT

A GLASS-BOX EXTENSION CAN MAKE YOUR WAKE!

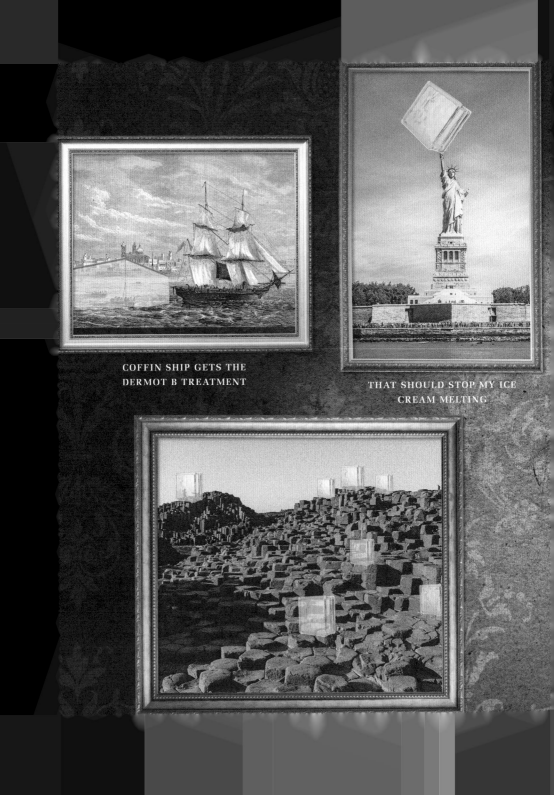

COFFIN SHIP GETS THE
DERMOT B TREATMENT

THAT SHOULD STOP MY ICE
CREAM MELTING

THAT SHOULD KEEP THE HIPPIES OUT

I WISH I WAS ON THE N17! STONE WALLS AND THE GLASS IS GREEN!

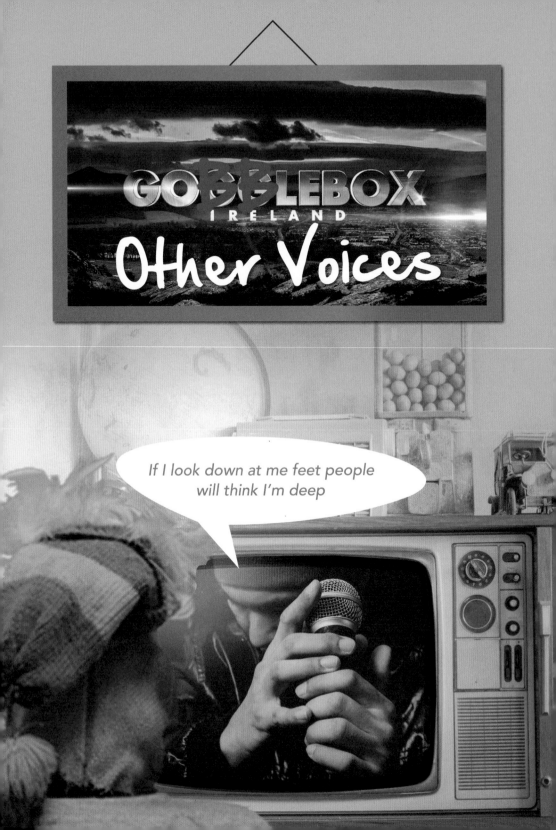

If watching Mass is your idea of great telly then *Other Voices* is one for you. The annual gathering of musical bed-wetters in crusty heaven Dingle airs on RTÉ2 every year at around 3am on Tuesdays in November. *Other Voices* is run by one of our nation's greatest ever spoofers, trad musician Philip King. The lad is quality when it comes to talking utter nonsense; if spoofing was on the Leaving Cert he'd have an A+++. Philip has been known to walk into rooms, tell people the Irish invented Rap and Reggae and leave with a grant. He's that good Fianna Fáil get him to give talks to their new members every year. A hard boss, he's been known to change presenters mid-interview. Last year's series had a total of 37 different presenters over six episodes.

At times it's hard to tell who's the interviewer and who's the interviewee as some girl with a cowboy hat, a beard and a tattoo of a glass of whiskey talks to some bloke with a cowboy hat, a beard and a tattoo of a glass of whiskey, both of them looking like they just got out of bed after seven weeks' sleep. This look is mainly due to the fact that both of them have just got out of bed after seven weeks' sleep.

Musicians talk in riddles designed to make the rest of us think they are deep and clever. Two years ago the amount of waffle talked at *Other Voices* got so big it ended up being served as breakfast in 79 of the 83 pubs in Dingle for eight months after the festival.

Things you are likely to see or hear on *Other Voices*:

1. Bands you've never heard of
2. Beards
3. Guitars
4. Vegans
5. Vegan beards with guitars in bands you've never heard of
6. Glen Hansard or someone else from The Frames with a fiddle
7. Singers looking at their sandals for entire songs
8. Singers with their eyes closed looking at the audience for entire songs
9. Bongos
10. A Hothouse Flower

Things you are unlikely to see or hear on *Other Voices*:

1. Bands you know
2. Songs you know
3. Songs you can hum
4. Someone not taking themselves too seriously
5. Joy
6. Craic
7. Laughter
8. Women without hairy armpits
9. Tans
10. Happy people

TOP TEN THINGS THAT SHOULD NEVER HAVE BEEN LET INTO IRELAND

Now that Theresa May has decided to build a wall between the Republic and Mexico (AKA Nordieland), it's time to reflect on a few things that should never have been let in in the first place.

1. COLDPLAY

Bog off and headline Bland Aid ya bunch of bed-wetters.

2. WATER TAX

That went well . . .

3. HIPSTERS

Only thing funnier than a hipster is a hipster from Cavan. Bog off with your vinyl-playing coffee bicycles made of hummus and take your beards, skinny jeans and fish-finger sangers with you.

4. IRELAND'S CALL

No one answering; let it go to voicemail.

5. MICHAEL FLATLEY

Didn't go great for the last lad who went around calling himself The Lord . . . fingers crossed.

6. THE POLISH

Coming over here, turning up for work on time, charging fair prices, not taking twelve tea-breaks a day and having hot motts. How are ordinary decent Irish builders meant to make a killing with them as competition?

7. AMERICAN FOOTBALL IN CROKE PARK

Time to bring that foreign games ban back in.

8. GARTH BROOKS

Giving boggers delusions and hope of a honkytonk life.

9. THE TROIKA

Coming over here taking our jobs, houses, money, food, water, good times and hope, and leaving us with our politicians.

10. THE BRITS

Coming over here and giving us a decent language, Trinity College, Parnell, coloured Polos, BBC1, the widow's pension, Adam Clayton, Def Leppard and Fine Gael.

Conor McFlatley
The Truth

After tirelessly unearthing the truth for WikiBeaks on behalf of the people of Ireland for well over three or four long hours a few weeks ago, I'd got to the point where I didn't really think I'd find anything that could shock me anymore. I mean, I've seen the minutes from the board meetings of The Gathering (yeah! I'd forgotten about that one too) and Irish Water (no, I hadn't forgotten about that one).

So, you can only imagine how I nearly tripped over my giblets when I discovered Tourism Ireland's top secret plan to build an Android Super-Irishman to unleash on the world, promoting Ireland and general Irishness, a global megastar bringing millions of visitors to the Emerald Isle and wowing the people of earth with incredible dancing and fighting skills. The name of this ultra-secret plot: Project Conor McFlatley.

This is the brainchild of Ethan Smith, a seven-year-old Dubliner who earlier this year was appointed as a Senior Special Advisor to the Minister for Tourism, Sports, Arts and Photo Ops. On his very first day in the department, Ethan, who says he was paid in 'homework off vouchers' from the Government, was delighted to learn that little-break was in fact an hour and a half long and immediately followed by big-break, which was three hours long. He used his little-break well: he drew a picture of Conor McFlatley. A senior

official spotted his drawing, had a light-bulb moment and there and then Ethan's drawing became the blueprint for the future of Irish tourism, as they were certain they'd found the perfect front person to win the hearts and minds of millions of tourists.

Senior Government Advisor Ethan Smith

things up the more they spent on it and the less homework I had to do.'

Ethan's not lying; this project has so far cost the Government €17 million which to date has generated Ethan's original drawing, 27 visits to Hong Kong, Silicon Valley and New York for 34 senior civil servants and their wives, and three failed prototypes, one of which loafed the Minister for Tourism in the head and kicked him in the shins simultaneously when he commented on his appearance.

After we shared our findings with the senior civil servant at the heart of the project, he accepted it had some 'teething problems'. He then asked if *we* got 'much homework' or if we had ever fancied seeing Hong Kong, Silicon Valley or New York.

Ever since getting a free GAA ref's whistle with a comic his Mum got him last week, Ethan has now become a committed whistleblower and so was very keen to fill me in on Project Conor McFlatley. 'I'm only seven and even I know my idea wasn't workable, but when someone is telling you ya can have homework off for the rest of the year, you just keep telling them how your crazy idea works . . . well, I'd be crazy not to keep making it up. The only problem was, these guys kept believing me and before I knew it they'd spent millions on trying to make it happen. I really thought, after how my electronic voting machine idea turned out, that they wouldn't keep listening to me but the truth is, the madder I made

For legal reasons we cannot continue this article. Also I'm a bit jet-lagged. I tell ya what, though, New York is some town.

RTÉ*GUIDE*DOGS

Win a week
at Crufts

Build your
own Kennel

**Labradoodle:
make up
your mind**

**Hug a
Pug week**

**Brian
Dogson**

The Woof
Guide to
the News

**The Mayo Rose
reveals her
competitive
streak: 'I do
like to Winalot'**

**George Hook Is
Barking Mad**

Lassie to join the cast of *Fair City*

WE CATCH UP WITH THE NEWSHOUND WITH A BONE TO PICK

Given his distinctive bark, it's no surprise that we hear Brian Dogson before we see him. On a call outside the RTÉ canteen the popular St Bernard is ordering his assistant to make sure she has his new red braces ready for our photo shoot and that the litter tray outside his kennel is covered with the *Irish Times*.

Once off the call Brian is polite and businesslike, asking us if we'd like to hear his thoughts on America's political future, the current situation in the Middle East or where he sees but in fairness he makes it feel like a week as he told us all about his pals Maccer, Fitzy, Doyler and Mahon who are all doing 'seriously well' over there and are a bunch of 'smashing guys'.

We try to get him back to our interview, suggesting he might let us know his thoughts on the latest *Fair City* storyline. At first it looks like he is biting but then it turned out he is literally biting as he clamps his gnashers onto my tape recorder and drools aggressively as he shakes it from side to side.

'Anne Doyle is the best anchorman I have worked with'

Ireland's place in a post-Brexit Europe. We explain that we're *The RTÉ Guide* and it'd probably just be best if he rattled off some guff about wanting to do *Dancing with the Stars*, Sharon Ní Bheoláin and any horror stories he has about Anne Doyle.

Brian looks at us with a black expression and begins an anecdote about a night out he had in London with some old college pals recently and how they believe that Britain is facing into blah, blah, blah . . . The, eh, story (?) goes on for a good hour

We decide at that point to park our next question about who he thinks will win *I'm A Celebrity* this year and instead let him tell us his thoughts on the challenges facing blah blah blah in a blah blah blah world.

It is riveting.

Brian Dogson will be appearing at the Dalkey-on-Thames Book Festival on Sat 11 June where he'll be reading extracts from his autobiography Woof Trade: Life as RTÉ's Top News Dog, *the follow-up to his best-selling* Woof Ride: The Day I Rode on the Redline Luas.

PIG

IN DUSTIUS WE TRUSTIUS

OP SE

PIGs FILE FOUR

THE DALKEY FILE
Dalkey – The Real Little Britain?

Of all the secret PIG files that we've uncovered here at WikiBeaks HQ, this one is both the most shocking and least surprising. For legal reasons we can't reveal our sources, but it definitely wasn't Sinn Féin or anyone in SIPTU.

A mysterious USB key left on my desk a few months ago exposes the plans of a secretive group known locally as 'The Dalkey Ski Club', plotted at clandestine gatherings on the ski slopes of Europe and the US.

The group, which does include one member who didn't go to Blackrock College (a boarder from Rockwell College whose sons are now all in Blackrock), has set out its mission – to ensure that Dalkey aligns its future with a post-Brexit Britain – via the following moves:

1. Changing its name officially to Dalkey-on-Thames.
2. Bidding to host the Commonwealth Games in 2022.
3. Inviting Queen Elizabeth to the Queens Pub to watch the rugger.
4. Renaming the Cuala GAA Club as The Oliver Cromwell Gaels and replacing football and hurling with rugger and cricket.
5. Rebranding the town's branch of Paddy Powers as Boris Powers.
6. Erecting statues of David McWilliams, David Drumm and Dave Kearney.
7. Turning the local Catholic church into an Educate Together school.
8. Including pesto with every bag of chips sold in the village chipper.
9. A ban on all cars more than one year old, all non-European cars and all non-SUV motors.
10. Running charity events for Children Without Skis, the Irish Pesto Institute and the Nigel Farage Centre For International Relations.

The Queens in Dalkey: Low on Harp . . . High on Heino

Cuala, the famous Dalkey GAA Club, soon to be renamed The Oliver Cromwell Gaels

Dalkey – where they clean their crisps

It's worth saying that they're not all up-themselves white-collar criminals born into privilege and just because it's home to some of this land's biggest bores doesn't mean there aren't some good heads there. I'm sure there are — there's a Paddy . . . sorry, a Boris Powers, a GAA . . . I mean a cricket club and a chipper so for every pesto-munching, SUV-driving, Dricco-licking, weekend Lycra-wearing 'great goy' cyclist, there must be a few sound lads too. But this latest file proves there are dark forces at work in Dalkey-on-Thames and for the protection of their neighbours in Sallynoggin, Ballybrack and Dun Laoghaire, it's crucial that we don't just stand by and let them take over.

Act now! Send what you can to Dustin, The Noggin, and I'll make sure we use your funds to fight the Evil Empire. Cash only.

(**Legal note: celebrity economist and general Brit-licker David McWilliams did not respond to questions on his alleged involvement in this group. As this is the first time in history that he has declined an interview about himself we can only assume that he DEFINITELY has nothing to do with this group. Nothing. At all. At all. Not a thing.**)

Camera-shy David McWilliams.

The Dalkey Masons – wink, wink . . . nudge, nudge

Preparations for St George's Day, biggest day of the year after the 12th of July in Dalkey

A useful way to spend the Queen's Shilling

Reasons why Aslan are better than U2

1. Far as I know, there's no Bono in Aslan.
2. Aslan have never snuck an album on to my phone.
3. If Aslan ever made enough to pay tax I'm sure they would pay it . . . oh wait, hang on . . . I might look that up on revenue.ie
4. Aslan didn't leg it to the Southside once they had a hit.
5. Aslan stayed true to the people of Ireland by refusing to have hits abroad.
6. Aslan take their humanitarian work very seriously, visiting Cork at least three times a year.
7. Christy cares so much about Aslan's hearing-impaired audience, he signs the words to all their songs at gigs.
8. Aslan have cleverly fought ticket scamming by touting their own tickets outside Aslan gigs.
9. Aslan's bass player can play the bass.

Aslan: Not Guilty

Bono tells Adam where to go

10. Aslan only had to have two hits to be loved. U2 had to have loads.

11. Aslan support the mighty Dubs by paying in to Croker. U2 only go near the place if they get a mighty fee.

12. Aslan play a hometown gig in Dublin at least once a year. U2 only play Amsterdam once every five years.

13. Aslan don't have silly nicknames like Bono, the Edge and Larry.

14. Aslan would fill bigger venues than U2 if most of their fans were not in prison.

15. Far as I know, U2 have never been brave enough to start a scrap with Linda Martin.

Aslan: Bravest band in the land

'LOOKS FEMALE,' SAYS DUSTIN

I'm not sure why vegans fancy me so much but I'm not complaining either as it's just great to have a mott turn me on outside of an oven. And I know when you picture a vegan most of the time you imagine a ginger mott with dreadlocks, a ukele and a dog on a piece of organic string walking through Shop Street in Galway singing 'Fisherman's Blues' but in fairness to Razz she's top-drawer hot. She claims to be from Tipperary which would make her the only female born in the county to look female in the last 100 years. Personally I think she may have been dropped off there by mistake as the aliens who built her were on their way to deliver her to a Miss Universe final and stopped in Tipp to catch a Declan Nerney gig.

Like most models, Razz talks a lot of crap but unlike lots of them she also eats a lot of crap too. And when I say crap, I mean actual crap. Though as it's organic, gluten-free, vegan crap she then takes pictures of it and calls herself a blogger/writer.

I tell you, if there's one thing that drives me mad it's celebrities shamelessly cashing in on their fame by releasing so-called books and then claiming to be authors. It's just so unfair to all those unpublished writers with actual talent who have to live in a world where anyone with a whiff of fame can get a book deal, while they have to get a job in a thing called 'a library', which is like a bookshop for book readers. It's an issue I've brought up time and time again with my publishers and one I'm determined to right.

Razz represented Ireland in Miss Universe in 2010 but was narrowly beaten by Miss Jupiter, who went on to marry event owner Donald J. Trump, a property developer from America who claims to be 'America's Bill Cullen'.

Splitting up with Razz wasn't much craic. Speaking of 'not much craic', she then went out with Bressie. I do hear from her from time to time and will always have a soft spot for her. Of all the Tipp vegan motts I've been linked with, she's defo in me top five and I wish her nothing but happiness as she continues to take over the media while she waits to receive her inheritance from the family's washing powder business.

THE BEGINNING

First broadcast in 1989, *Fair City* is Ireland's longest-running comedy. For the first two years the show used actors but this was stopped due to the cast turning up with cravats, berets, pipes and notions and the actors were promptly replaced with people walking past RTÉ. Nobody noticed the difference. In the early years, *Fair City* suffered from not being as popular as the much-loved hit rural soap *Glenroe* so RTÉ management came up with a cunning plan and axed their much-loved hit show to help its not-so-loved one. It's that kind of genius thinking that has helped make RTÉ what it is today.

CARRIGSTOWN

The soap is set in the fictional area of Carrigstown (which is Latin for 'town made of plywood') and is meant to look like a typical urban town but instead looks like a TV soap opera set made in 1980s Romania. Many fans have been shocked to discover that if you enter Carrigstown into a sat-nav the voice tells you to 'get a life'.

STORYLINES

In 2006, *Fair City* gave us a storyline that . . . oh sorry, that should just read: 'In 2006, *Fair City* gave us a storyline.'

UNIONS

In 2012 unions in RTÉ demanded that a Spar shop be put on the set so they wouldn't have to leave the campus to get their breakfast rolls.

BUDGET

The makers of the show plan to cut costs by bringing *Love/Hate's* Nidge in to run the community centre and bring down costs by murdering half the cast.

PRODUCTION

There is none.

McCoy's pub following a major refurbishment by RTÉ

GERMANS

In 2010, as part of the Troika bailout, Angela Merkel demanded that *Fair City* go from two nights to four nights a week, saying, 'You deserve this, you potato-eating, Riverdancing leprechauns. You sold the family silver and now you must suffer more Paul Brennan, Neasa Dillon and Bela Doyle.' Poor Greece has it six nights a week and an omnibus on Sunday.

THEME SONG

In fairness to the clowns that make this muck, they have managed to compose the only opening and closing theme that nobody remembers, despite over 5,000 airings.

LIFE AFTER THE SOAP

Scriptwriters have ingenious ways of getting rid of characters:

Robin McKenna moved to Cork 'for a job'.

Robert Daly moved to Belfast 'for a job'.

Jennifer Conway moved to Galway 'for a job'.

Ian Walsh moved to Mayo 'for a job'.

Kay Costello moved to Limerick 'for a job'.

THE FUTURE

The Carrigstown drama will tackle many controversial and taboo issues next year with plans to have Mondo buying pasta instead of rice in the local Spar before moving to Tipperary for a job.

kipAdvisor®

New Ross   Hotels   Flights   Holiday Rentals   Restaurants

Find: Things to Do

New Ross

SO GOOD THEY NAMED IT ONCE

New Ross has a vibrant and innovative community that values its natural environment and preserves its heritage. It has a thriving economy and is home to some of the world's most VBPs (very beautiful people). But that, of course, is New Ross, Nova Scotia, Canada; by contrast, New Ross in Wexford is a prize kip.

On the approach to New Ross is the town's coat of arms, which depicts two lads kicking the crap out of one another outside the chipper, with the town's Latin motto, *'defacto erratum quid pro quo'* meaning 'where 30% of the locals are toilet trained'.

The earliest settlement in this area dates back to the sixth century when St Abban of Mugheranoidhe founded a monastery in the town (which is now a Spar), St Abban is the patron saint of lost causes, BO and Marrying your Cousin.

New Ross, like the rest of Wexford, has a strong association with Strongbow, drinking more of the famous cider than any other county. New Ross's most celebrated son is the 35th President of United States of America, John Fitzgerald Kennedy, whose great-grandfather Patrick Kennedy emigrated from New Ross in 1849. JFK visited New Ross in June 1963. Reports say that he was so traumatised and embarrassed by what he saw on his visit that he went home to the States and arranged to have himself assassinated in Dallas in November of the same year. A statue of JFK is located on the quayside of the town and you can regularly see locals throwing bread at it from the nearby grassy knoll.

Literacy and parking are crippling New Ross

Europe > Ireland > Province of Leinster > County of Wexford > **New Ross Tourism**

RAIL
The railway station closed on 30 March 1964 though it was only March this year that the final passenger died on the platform waiting for a train.

New Ross University

Hartford to take legal action

As New Ross is still going through the famine, the people of the town decided to build a replica famine ship (or pleasure cruiser as they call it), the *Dunbrody*.

ECONOMIC ACTIVITY
Picking strawberries.

ROADS
A €230m deal has been agreed for the construction of a 13.6 km bypass of New Ross (money well spent).

New Ross nite life

The latest reviews. **The lowest prices.** The perfect place . . .

Things to Do   Forum   Best of 2017   More

COMMENTS

Search

"Five-a-day"
◎◎◎◎◎ Reviewed 1 days ago   NEW

'Asbestos has to be one of their five-a-day'

Sophie from Wellington

"RUN"
◎◎◎◎◎ Reviewed 2 days ago   NEW

'RUN'

Thomas from Quebec

"Buy a return ticket"
◎◎◎◎◎ Reviewed 16 days ago   NEW

'My advice: if you're visiting this Kip,
buy a return ticket'

Delta from Adelaide

"Perfect"
◎◎◎◎◎ Reviewed 21 days ago   NEW

'Don't blame me – no one's perfect'

God from everywhere

Famous bird-fancier JFK

kennedyhomestead.ie

The Kennedy Homestead

Shoot me now

WIKIBEAKS   119

PATRICK P. KENNY

If you were to name all the truly great people of the world since time began and I mean *the truly great*, you could possibly count them on one hand. That makes five (or six if you're from Cavan). I remember putting a simple list together as I started my career in television:

Jesus

Mahatma Gandhi

Aung San Suu Kyi

Martin Luther King

Shakira Shakira

I don't think too many people would disagree with my list, except maybe Martin Luther King, as after his brilliant work on the Civil Rights Movement he went and ballsed it up with his brutal presenting on the *Six O'Clock Show*. But then again, no one is perfect, not even me – yes, NOT even me. I may be gorgeous, funny, amazing singing voice, etc., but I have to confess: this Turkey is flawed. The greatest person of all was not on my list.

THE BEGINNING

As I walked the corridors of RTÉ to my first week on *The Den*, I remember people pointing, going 'That's him, that's Dustin the Turkey. He's going to help save Zig and Zag's ailing career, he's just so funny.' 'I wonder if he's single?' asked a young Sharon Ní Bheoláin. This continued for months, years even. I'm not going to lie to you – I loved the compliments, the notoriety. But all was not well in camp Dustin because no matter how good I was, how many viewers I had, how many number ones I had, there was always someone better than me, and the truth is, folks, there always will be.

Pat's Gaff: he put a lot of himself into this

Patrick P. Kenny was born on 29 January 1948 in Lough Key Forest. His Dad was a sycamore and his Mum a silver birch. Pat Kenny is a broadcasting genius – there, I said it. So why did I slag, ridicule, torment this giant of television? Because I was jealous.

LEGEND OF BROADCASTING

Gay Byrne, Johnny Carson, Michael Parkinson, Oprah, Letterman, Socky and Norton all learnt their presenting skills from Mr P; we all did. Pat started his career modelling for a timber floor company when RTÉ spotted him filming an advert. He quickly shot up the ladder (a cousin of his) with shows like *Kenny Live*, *The Frontline* and *Prime Time*. In 1999, as a present to the world to celebrate the new Millennium, Pat was given *The Late Late Show*. RTÉ cleverly used some lad called Gay Byrne for 37 years as a warm-up for our genius, who was about to make television history by forgetting his first ever guest's name (true) and showing off his ability to make a nation feel awkward and want to hide behind their sofas anytime he did 'entertainment'. The Plank made the famous *Toy Show* his own by never engaging with the kids, kicking the toys around the studio and looking at his watch every two minutes while sweating buckets of sap. Pat refused to wear the traditional, fun, colourful, woolly jumper, instead opting for a navy sweatshirt you would see a lad wear if you brought your car to an exhaust centre.

The Late Late Toy Show, *highlight of every child's Christmas*

BRANCHING OUT

In 2009, one year after earning €950,956 from RTÉ, Plank left Gay Byrne's *Late Late Show*. Brian Cowen, the Taoiseach at the time, announced a national day of mourning. But worse was to come. On that fateful day, 31 July 2013, we all know where we were when we heard the devastating news that Pat was to leave RTÉ. Riots broke out worldwide, political leaders begged this genius to rethink his decision. Light did appear at the end of the tunnel as the Plank was not ready for the old sawmill just yet, and was simply moving to the brilliant, amazing, innovative UTV Ireland, where he would interview guests in the round like Lulu (me neither) and ask questions like: 'Do you still enjoy singing?' and 'Do you come from a musical background?' Genius.

OLIVE BRANCH

Sporty Pat

I was sitting at home in the Noggin with the Seoige sisters one Tuesday evening when the phone rang, I answered and heard Christmas is coming and you're going to get a big stuffing. I was about to say 'Very funny, Al Porter,' when I heard creaking on the other end of the line. I knew it was him: the Guru of the media, Mr Friday Night, the King of Television, the man who interviewed Lulu (still me neither) – Pat 'the Plank' Kenny. 'Hey, Justin,' said that rough-hewn voice, 'why don't we do a groovy cappuccino? I'd love you to interview me.' I was trembling: Pat was talking to me. 'But, Pat, are you sure? I said some terrible things about you – like when you go on holidays you use Cuprinol as sun cream.' 'All in the past, little buddy,' he replied. 'Thanks Pat,' I said. 'Let's bury the hatchet.' (Sorry, couldn't resist.)

So that's how I got to interview the most amazing person that has ever set foot on planet earth: the man, the legend, Pat Kenny.

Pat visits his granddad

INTERVIEW

Dustin: What's your proudest moment?

Pat: Tying the knot with Kathy. I met her on the dating website Timber.

Dustin: What type of clothes do you like to wear?

Pat: Trunks.

Dustin: What's your favourite animal sound?

Pat: Bark.

Dustin: What do you like to eat?

Pat: Chips.

Dustin: Why do you change shows so often?

Pat: Because I get board and sometimes I like to branch out and turn over a new leaf.

Two legends, together for the first time

What an honour to interview the virtuoso the Plank Kenny.

The cabinet are proposing to celebrate the genius of the man by having a national Pat Kenny day, it will be on March 17th and simply known as Patrick's Day.

Pardon Me, Micky D.

Readers! I know millions of you are keen to help me. I've lost count of how often complete strangers have come up to me and said, 'Dustin, you're amazing. You make Ireland a better place and without you there would be little for us to be proud about. You inspire us to be better people. Is there any way we can repay you for everything you've done for our nation? Would you like money?'

Well, here is your chance to do something for me, with this special 'cut out'n'send' letter to President Micky D. Higgins asking him to grant me an official pardon. The lad claims to be a humanitarian (I don't eat humans meself but there's no judging going on here) but in a world where a clown like Trump manages to find it in his heart to spare a turkey every year I believe our President should do the right thing and spare me.

I know once the millions of you who've bought this book send him the special cut-out letter printed overleaf, my Christmases will be saved forever, and I'll no longer have to hide in fear of Paxo.

Poultry Power!

President Micky D. Higgins,
Arás An Ucturasomethingorother,
Beside The Zoo,
Phoenix Park,
Dubalin 1.

Dear Micky D,

As a citizen of Ireland I am calling on you, the President of Ireland, to exercise your right and issue a pardon to Dustin the Turkey.

As you know, every Christmas thousands of Dustin's cousins are cruelly served up for dinner and leftovers.

Plucked and then stuffed in a barbaric fashion, these innocent birds are delicious, but given the incredible contribution Dustin has made to Irish life over the last couple of decades I believe you should use your immense powers to spare him the indignity of spending every Christmas on the run and hiding out in various pantos.

The choice is yours, Micky D., and yours alone, but remember if Dustin does end up on someone's Christmas table it'll be you who'll have to face a nation in mourning and explain that it didn't have to be this way. Trust me, no 'poem' is going to get you out of this one.

Love to Sabrina ('Boys! Boys! Boys!' was a classic!).

Yours etc.,

....

Insert name here.

Acknowledgements

Dustin's *WikiBeaks*
Typed for Dustin The Turkey
by Johnny Morrison and Darren Smith

Massive thanks to Eoin McHugh for having the smarts not to publish the first idea, going for this one and then legging it before the blame starts. This book is still largely your fault, Eoin.

Brian Langan, there are no words . . . or at least there were no words, and certainly none that were spelt correctly, until you came along. This book will be your publishing legacy and there's nothing you can do about it. You've no one to blame but yourself and your endless patience for doing such a great job. The biscuits are on us.

Huge thanks also to Bobby Birchall for the mega design work.

Fiona Murphy, we know your PR skills will be the reason this book becomes the global smash you've said it's destined to become, so thanks in advance.

To Ray D'Arcy, my mentor and giver of golden advice. As you say, Ray, 'What goes on tour between a grown man and an Elf in Lapland stays on tour.'

Zig and Zag! I forgive you for turning your back on the children of Éire in search of the Queen's shilling. Hope it was worth it and that your best friend Chris Evans is still there for you.

To all in RTÉ, you're in my thoughts and prayers. Take comfort from the old saying: 'Someday this will all be over'. In the meantime, have hope, be brave . . . and remember: never, ever make a decision.

Thanks also to Kyran O'Brien for the pics, Jenny Smith for the camera, Ethan Smith for the drawing, Roz Purcell, Aslan, and to booksellers and bookshops for putting this book where it belongs.

WikiBeaks is dedicated to big kids everywhere and to the 'people' of Leitrim.

Picture Acknowledgements

Every effort has been made to contact copyright holders where known. Those who have not been acknowledged are invited to get in touch with the publishers.

All photos featuring Dustin are courtesy of the authors with the exception of the following: pp. 2–3, 28 (top), 56, 58, 66–8 all © Kyran O'Brien. All KipAdvisor, Dalkey and Patrick P. Kenny photos are courtesy of the authors with the exception of the following Shutterstock images: pp. 36 (right) and 109 (bottom). Drawing on p. 102 by Ethan Smith. Photo of Ethan Smith on p. 103 courtesy of his mother. Photo on p. 110 courtesy of Aslan. Photo on p. 112 courtesy of Roz Purcell. Photos on the following pages are courtesy of RTÉ Archives: pp. 10, 11, 111 (bottom), 115. Gogglebox Ireland logo courtesy of Kite Entertainment.

All other images are from Shutterstock apart from the following: p. 9 © Carolina Biological Supply Company; p. 14 (E Street Band) © Anthony Correia / Shutterstock, (Mother Teresa) © Manfredo Ferrari; p. 22 (Edge) © Jaguar PS / Shutterstock; p. 30 © Featureflash Photo Agency / Shutterstock; p. 40 (Trump) © Marina Linchevska / Shutterstock; p. 42 (Van) © S. Bukley / Shutterstock; p. 51 (top) © Krista Kennell / Shutterstock; p. 51 (middle): Rihardzz / Shutterstock; p. 51 (bottom) © Creative Lab / Shutterstock; p. 54 © Jaguar PS / Shutterstock; pp. 66-69 (background) © Marianna Ianovska / Shutterstock; p. 69 (bottom) © Photomaster2000 / Shutterstock; pp. 73–74 © Featureflash Photo Agency / Shutterstock; p. 76 © Jaguar PS / Shutterstock; p. 83 © EML / Shutterstock; p. 89 (left) © Rolf G Wackenberg / Shutterstock, (top) © Alessia Pierdomenico / Shutterstock; p. 125 (top) © Rihardzz / Shutterstock.